Collins

Negotiation Skills

IN **7**

SIMPLE STEPS

Collins

HarperCollins Publishers
77-85 Fulham Palace Road
Hammersmith
London W6 8JB

First edition 2014
10 9 8 7 6 5 4 3 2 1
© HarperCollins Publishers 2014
ISBN 978-0-00-750721-4

The Publisher and author wish to thank the following rights holders for the use of
copyright material: With thanks to Twitter for the use of Twitter and Tweet. If any
copyright holders have been omitted, please contact the Publisher who will make the
necessary arrangements at the first opportunity.
Illustrations by Scott Garrett.

MIX
**Paper from
responsible sources**
FSC™ C007454
FSC
www.fsc.org

FSC™ is a non-profit international organisation established to promote the
responsible management of the world's forests. Products carrying the FSC
label are independently certified to assure consumers that they come from
forests that are managed to meet the social, economic and ecological needs
of present and future generations, and other controlled sources.

Find out more about HarperCollins and the environment at
www.harpercollins.co.uk/green

Contents

About the author

Clare Dignall has worked in both the public and private sectors, in established organizations and challenging start-ups. Since working for herself, she has realized – more so than ever – the importance of forming close business relationships and extending her network. When authoring this book, Clare used material from Barry Tomalin's *Key Business Skills* (HarperCollins 2012) in addition to bouncing ideas off Joe Cairney of Projects on Track, who Clare would like to thank for his insights and enthusiasm. Clare is also the author of the HarperCollins title *Can You Eat, Shoot & Leave?*, the official companion to Lynne Truss's bestseller *Eats, Shoots & Leaves,* as well as Collins *Successful Networking in 7 Simple Steps.*

Step 1
UNDERSTANDING NEGOTIATION METHODS

'No question is ever settled until it's settled right.'
— Ella Wheeler Wilcox (1850–1919), Poet

Five ways to succeed

- Negotiate to invest in relationships, not to damage them.
- Recognize how frequently you negotiate in everyday life.
- Always ensure there is enough time for negotiations.
- Identify what you can concede to help reach agreement.
- Learn as much as you can about your opposite number.

Five ways to fail

- Take up a fixed negotiating position, and don't give in.
- Use the methods that have worked for you before.
- Don't waste time planning; spontaneity gets results.
- Never build relationships before negotiations.
- Don't assign team roles; let everyone speak equally.

What is negotiation?

Hear the word 'negotiation' and you'll probably imagine sharp-suited executives haggling across a gleaming boardroom table, or millionaire footballers hammering out transfer deals with big-name clubs. Whatever comes to mind, it's unlikely that the images you come up with are of people just like you. Inexplicably, we associate the word 'negotiation' with people who are rich and powerful: that negotiating is something we'll never have to do. But that's just the thing; we negotiate all the time, every one of us, with varying success.

So, if it's not just boardroom stuff, what is it? At its core, negotiation is nothing more than a dialogue between two or more parties working towards making an agreement, resolving a conflict, or reaching mutually beneficial goals. Sound familiar? In fact, you've probably negotiated a couple of times before lunch today already. In its most common guise, negotiation is the simple process of explaining your needs, exploring options and reaching agreement in ways that make life more navigable. At its most strategic, these basic tactics are formalized into standard procedures that can, for example, help businesses work together, help ambassadors improve international relations, and in the direst circumstances, save the lives of prisoners and hostages.

Why should we negotiate?

In an effort to appear easy-going, we may often avoid speaking out for the things that we want or need from life, whether that be in personal relationships or in our working lives. This means we'll avoid negotiation, because it just doesn't feel natural. Many of us assume that negotiating will jeopardize ongoing relationships with a loved one, or with an employer. But in many cases, this assumption is wrong, and avoiding negotiation means everyone loses: the partner in a relationship who never voices their needs may be taken for granted and decide to leave; the single parent who won't ask for flexible working may end up quitting a good job for a dead-end one that better fits the school day. But by careful negotiation, such endings can be avoided. The key is identifying, and striving for, areas of mutual advantage that will allow everyone to benefit in some way (often called a win-win situation). If this happens, both relationships can emerge intact, or even improved. Negotiating needn't necessarily entail conflict; there may be tough moments on the way to resolution, but by negotiating the problem side by side, you're actually investing in the future relationship, rather than damaging it.

Different negotiation environments

Though we negotiate constantly in our daily lives, the prospect of negotiating at work can still be terrifying. If you're feeling like this, it's worthwhile looking closer at everyday negotiation environments and noting how they use repeated and recognizable processes. Acknowledging these skills you've developed 'off-duty' can help you build a portfolio of negotiation experience to apply in the workplace.

Resolving conflict

To successfully resolve disputes we create a setting in which each party can air their grievances objectively. Both sides must try not to let anger cloud the issues, because 'getting personal' just doesn't help. Both may then explain the areas they find unreasonable. Exploring how the dispute has come about and developed is an important step in preventing recurrence. Having identified the problem, it's time to propose solutions for mutual benefit. Facing conflict promptly is central to resolution. This may sound like a complex set of procedures, but it's likely you've navigated them a thousand times, whether resolving an argument with your partner, or agreeing the line of a boundary fence with your neighbour. Next time you resolve conflict at home, note the actions you undertook, and consider how you might use them in the workplace.

Making decisions

A negotiated decision's central premise is that you are trying to reach a decision that's 'better' than would have been possible without negotiating. Say you have to agree with another team from your office on a new software package that you both need. To reach a decision, both sides must research options to understand the choice and availability, and agree the selection criteria they'll use, so it's clear the final choice will be a fair one. Then they need to identify constraints, as some packages may not have all the features each team needs. Both parties may need to make concessions – perhaps sacrificing a desirable software add-on to keep the purchase affordable for everyone. Sound complicated? You're more experienced in this than you think. These are the exact processes we undertake to make the simplest decisions – where to eat, when to take a holiday, what colour to paint our living rooms.

Buying

Buying in the workplace can take many forms, from purchasing contractor services to hiring staff. The buyer must identify the needs of all interested parties, agree available budget and schedule, and research the options that meet the majority of these needs most effectively. At the point of purchase, and if the time is right, the buyer may even haggle, on price perhaps, or try to get an 'added extra' that sweetens the deal. It's worth remembering that these procedures are the very same we undertake when making a big personal purchase, such as buying a house, a car, or a holiday.

Selling

Successful selling depends on how well we know our product and our market. Whether punting vintage comics on eBay, or leftover lawn turf to a colleague for cash; the vendor must know what their product or service provides in terms of benefits, and what competitors charge, before they can arrive at a fair price. How does this apply to negotiation? Take this skill-set and apply it, for example, to negotiating for better pay, which is, in blunt terms, 'selling' the product of you at market value, and not a penny below it.

Many skills needed for successful negotiation are ones that we apply in our daily lives, probably without noticing. By taking this tool kit, extending and formalizing it a little, we can approach negotiation in our working lives too. Whether you seek to advance your career or get a good deal from suppliers, believe it or not, you're already surprisingly well-equipped.

RAIN MACS
FOR SALE
£5

Knowing when to negotiate

While developing your negotiation skills is invaluable, it's just as important to know when it's appropriate to negotiate and when it's not a good idea. Recognizing when negotiation isn't an option will save you time, effort, and credibility.

Do both (or more) parties have something to gain?

To negotiate, you and your opposite number must have some common ground to work from, and both must have something to gain.

Do you want to stick around?

Do you want to have a future relationship with the other party? If so, negotiation is the best option, because if you don't share your needs, one or both of you will walk away.

Do you and the other party (or parties) have time?

If time is short, and you can't postpone negotiation, you'll be unable to prepare effectively enough to achieve much. You wouldn't choose a holiday in 90 seconds, so it's unlikely you'll successfully negotiate better pay on finding yourself in the lift with your boss.

If you open negotiations while the other party is under pressure at work or home, you risk an abrupt response because they need to keep proceedings short.

First steps

Perhaps the most pivotal aspect of negotiation beyond all others is preparation. By preparing for every negotiation on an individual basis, you'll boost your chances of reaching a satisfactory resolution, starting here:

Set a primary 'gut feeling' objective

Before you even start to research the market or set of circumstances in which you're negotiating, write down what you would want to achieve in an ideal-world scenario. This will focus your research efforts and provide clarity for the road ahead. Look back at this objective any time that you feel your negotiation proceedings are getting lost in detail.

Make time to gather knowledge

Only by preparing properly will you be able to gather enough information about your opposite number, and the issue under discussion, to give your negotiations authority and credibility. In the next few pages we'll look at preparatory research in depth.

Never assume what worked before will work again

If you've negotiated before, and with success, it's forgivable to assume that you'll do the same again by applying the same tactics. But, every negotiation is unique – even one new face or a different deadline in the mix can hugely alter the objectives.

Know what you want

Once you've identified your ideal objective, which can be as simple as 'get myself a pay rise', you should examine what it is you *really* want – in detail. Here are a few examples to get you started:

- What do I/we want to get as a result of the negotiations?

- What would the perfect deal be?

- What would an acceptable deal be?

- When do I/we want or need negotiations to start and finish?

- What are my/our financial limits/aspirations?

- How important is the ongoing relationship with the other party?

- How long can I/we wait for delivery of the agreed item/terms?

Asking yourself or your team these questions will help you identify acceptable alternatives to the 'perfect deal', or note some aspects that you'd be willing to trade off. What is key in identifying what you want is not establishing a determined, immovable 'position', but what your specific interests really are. Knowing what these interests are will provide you with much more material to negotiate with than creating a fixed stance over which the only choice is to haggle aggressively. Noting these interests is also the first step in creating your negotiation strategy.

Know what you can give

After identifying what your specific interests are, ask yourself and/or your team some open questions to reveal just how little or how much you're prepared to bargain. Everyone must agree on these terms wholeheartedly, and stick to them. Here are just a few examples of the type of questions you may ask:

■ Could I/we wait for a better sale price/a bigger payrise in the longer term?

■ Could I accept home working in place of a car allowance?

■ Could I accept more annual leave instead of a bonus this year?

But how can 'giving in' suit both parties? Surely you're losing out? Not necessarily, because the analysis process can reveal some unexpected interests you didn't know you had. You may, for example, realize that an immediate bonus rather than a later pay rise would suit you because you're getting married and don't want to take out a loan for the wedding. You're happy: your employer is delighted. Analysing what you *really* want and what you're willing to give are the first foundations of your negotiation strategy, and will provide you with materials that can be discussed and traded off to reach a resolution that potentially benefits both (or more) parties.

Know your USP

One part of your preparatory jigsaw still needs to be slotted into place. This is your USP, your 'unique selling proposition'; the hook that will keep your opposite number interested in you and in reaching a good resolution, no matter how long the negotiation.

What is a USP?

The unique selling proposition is a marketing term which describes the qualities that only you can provide, or provide best, compared to all other competitors. The USP concept doesn't just apply to negotiations related to buying and selling; ever-increasingly you'll need to emphasize your USP in job interviews, and in negotiations for pay or promotion.

Recognize your USP

Whether negotiating as a team or one to one, you'll have to know your USP. What can you offer that no one else can? What is it that makes you unique and sought after? Crucially, it must be an attribute that's important to the other party, or your USP will be irrelevant. To identify your USP fully, you must consider it in terms of what your opposite party needs. When the time comes to research them, think carefully about what it is you could offer to respond uniquely to their requirements.

Get ready to sell your USP

Having a convincing selling proposition will help you counter most, if not all, challenges. For example, a proven ability to provide support across a number of office roles or, for suppliers, award-winning customer service will help counter statements such as 'Liz has been here longer than you and isn't asking for a raise' or 'we know another supplier who can undercut your costs'. When a USP offers an intangible but compelling concept of added value, it's difficult for your opposite number to dismiss it, even against tangible factors such as price.

When you've determined your USP, it's important that you're comfortable talking about it, even before you begin negotiations. Take a little time to craft your USP into a short statement of no more than 20 clear, credible words. If you're going into team negotiations, make sure every team member is comfortable with it, understands it, (believes it!) and can justify it if asked.

Know your opposite number

No matter what the circumstance, whether a neighbourhood campaign against a new road or negotiating for better working conditions in a factory, research will help you shape your negotiation strategy and help you make an educated guess about what the other party's strategy will be too.

Gather all possible information

Ask the other party who they plan to field: Providing your opposite number knows you're about to enter into negotiations with them, they should expect to be asked for such information. Ask who will be present, what their job titles are, and brief background information about them. Ask who'll be leading, what roles the others will fulfil, and offer the same in return.

Search LinkedIn® and other social media: Now you've got names, explore their career profiles on LinkedIn® to discover their special interests and skills. Finding their profile page on Facebook or Twitter may uncover nuggets about likes and dislikes, hobbies and aspirations. This could give you common ground from which to build a relationship, or provide a talking point to ease a tense coffee break. And simply knowing what the other team looks like will help you fit names to faces quickly on the day, making you appear confident and attentive.

Check their company website: If you're negotiating with representatives of a company, you should check the company website for information such as claimed service standards and company ethos. Being able to point out a mismatch between what they say during negotiations and what they claim on their site may give you some leverage.

Read their publications: Most company websites will hold newsletters, annual reports, and staff magazines in pdf form. Annual reports provide financial information that can reveal, for example, any debts, expansion plans, and the company's financial targets for the year. If you know they're in debt, for example, this could put you into the driving seat of negotiations, as you know they'll be keen to work quickly to save money. If, on the other hand, you're being interviewed for a job and plan to negotiate your starting salary upwards, then quoting their staff magazine on how crucial recruitment is to the health of the company may also make them sit up and take notice.

Talk to their customers: Whether a big corporate or a one-man band, most companies are proud to list important clients on their website. Do you know anyone listed there? Can they tell you about their experiences of working with the person or company you're interested in? Take some time to catch up with these contacts. If it feels appropriate, they might be willing to provide insights into their own negotiations with the company you're dealing with, or mention any customer service shortfalls they've experienced.

Profile the people: Whether it's one person or a whole team, you now have an idea of their career path, likes, dislikes, common contacts, and any shared interests. By digesting their LinkedIn® profile (especially their recommendations) you may also build up a picture of their workplace strengths and style. Facebook and others may reveal glimpses of temperament and personality. It's good to know in advance if you're coming to table with a tough negotiator, and equally useful to know if your opposite number is inexperienced, which can make for both easy, or unpredictable, negotiations.

Profile the company: Look for common company objectives that could provide potential for joint gains. Perhaps they aspire to becoming more 'green' and your cleaning service uses eco-detergents and recycling as standard? Perhaps they plan to gain more local clients to cut back on travel costs, and you're slap bang in their neighbourhood. What are their published service standards compared to what customers tell you? Explaining that you're aware of a shortfall could give you valuable negotiation leverage.

Get to know each other

Establishing a preliminary relationship before negotiating may instil a glimmer of mutual trust. Email to arrange negotiations dates, venues and teams. Vary your contact – if they're coming to you, email to confirm arrangements, then make a friendly call later to check if they've additional needs on the day, like a flipchart or veggie sandwiches. Keeping contact regular and approachable makes the prospect of meeting at the negotiation table much less daunting.

Know your team

While many of your negotiating experiences will be one to one, there may be times when you feel it's better to bring helpers to the table with you. But when?

When is it best to use a team?

To represent the interests of many: Where the welfare of many is at stake, e.g. in neighbourhoods, local councils, retail, construction, call-centres and factories, a team of individuals who each represent a constituent group can better reflect their diverse needs.

When you need to think differently: Where negotiations are complex, where there seems no way of reaching a mutually beneficial result, or if a one-to-one negotiation has already broken down, it's time to bring in the collective imagination of a team.

To show that this is important: Turning up in number is a concise way of saying this is important to you. For example, a team would underline the depth of community feeling if fielded against a construction company surveying parkland. However, turning up mob-handed on your neighbour's doorstep to discuss his hedge, or arriving to talk pay with your boss flanked by colleagues, will look aggressive. If it's important *only to you,* then it's usual that only you should turn up.

How to choose your team

If you plan to field a team in negotiations, it's crucial that your own people don't throw you any curve balls – there will be enough surprises coming from your opposite party. Consider the following steps when selecting your negotiating team.

1 Choose members wisely: If you're negotiating in a particular field, you may want a specialist in that topic on your team to advise. If you have to talk money and pricing, you'll want someone who's good – and fast – with numbers. If possible, don't include anyone, no matter how close you are, who you suspect may be a weak link. If they're being pressed upon you by your boss, ensure that person understands that, during the negotiation, it's the lead negotiator who's in charge, not the boss.

2 Ensure they understand the issues, and each other: Before going into negotiations as a team, it's imperative that your team know why you want to negotiate, that they understand how you came to this decision (and support it), and that they know each other really well. You don't want an unpredictable member of your team suddenly asking you, in front of the opposite party, to clarify why negotiations are needed.

3 Have a proper discussion: Make time with your fledgling team to brainstorm the issues you want to air during negotiations, including the 'what we want' and 'what we can give' options. Agree both on what information you are willing to share with the opposing party, and what you must not mention in front of them.

Matching your team to negotiation roles

The next step in creating an effective team is to assign its members with discrete roles. Although specialisms are important, you're not just looking for professional or technical skills, but personality traits too. Maybe you know someone who is unflappable in a crisis, or a people-person who makes others feel at ease. Experience is crucial too; a tough-nut negotiator who has been through this before is a great asset – if you know of one!

Your team may include as few as two of the following roles, or it may include all of them and more.

■ **Lead negotiator:** This spokesperson for the team makes the tough decisions and does most of the talking, as well as organizing and motivating the team.

■ **A note-taker:** Someone needs to impartially record the key agreements being made. There need only be one 'scribe' in a negotiation, so it's good to agree early which party will provide one.

■ **An observer:** For big negotiations, there can be merit in having someone who can watch for signs of anxiety or resentment in the other party, and can share these insights in breaks or between meetings.

■ **A numbers person:** If you're negotiating about buying, selling, or pay, for example, you may need someone who has a head for numbers, spreadsheets and forecasting.

■ **An expert adviser:** If you're negotiating about one aspect in a specialist field, e.g. conservation, you may want someone who can bring expert insight to your strategy and who can answer complex questions with authority.

Know your authorities

Ensure that your people know that they can't make proposals or counter offers over the lead negotiator, unless it's been discussed in advance. Also, if the lead doesn't have the power of 'sign-off', then you should make it clear from the outset that any agreements reached will have to be passed by the person who does have the authority. Being vague about this could irritate the other party and cause delay.

Decide how you'll communicate

Consider whether to agree a set of discreet signals to communicate important things you may be unable to say out loud e.g.: 'I disagree'; 'stop talking'; 'change the topic'; or 'we need a break to talk'. Once you've got your signals, practise using them together until you can decipher them with confidence. If you need to say something specific, writing a note and pushing it under the eyes of a team member is acceptable too.

Key take-aways

Write down the things you will take away from Step 1 and how you will implement them.

Topic	Take-away	Implementation
Understanding that negotiation is a part of everyday life	• *I negotiate every day both at home and in the office.*	• *Bring some of the skills I use at home into the office environment.*
Understanding why we should negotiate		
Identifying negotiation skills already gained in everyday negotiating environments		
How to recognize when it's a good time to negotiate		
How to prepare effectively for a negotiation		
How to identify what you want from negotiation		
How to identify what you can give to achieve results		
How to recognize your USP and use it effectively in negotiation		
How to recognize when a team might work well		
How to choose the right team		
How to assign roles to your team		

Step 2

PREPARE YOUR STRATEGY

'By failing to prepare, you are preparing to fail.'
— Benjamin Franklin, (1704–1790), Politician,
Inventor and Scientist

Five ways to succeed

- Create a flexible and researched negotiation strategy.
- Be clear about what you want to gain.
- Make an educated guess about the other party's strategy.
- Dress appropriately and comfortably.
- Be positive and friendly when you arrive.

Five ways to fail

- Allow your walk-away points to change during a negotiation.
- Always assume you have the least leverage.
- Don't rehearse your strategy – be spontaneous.
- Insist on negotiating at your chosen venue.
- Speak very loudly to appear more confident.

Create your negotiation strategy

You've spent valuable time preparing for negotiations: gathering information and identifying what you want and what you can concede to reach a satisfactory agreement. Now it's time to distil your efforts into a negotiation strategy: not a fixed plan, but a flexible guideline of what you hope to achieve and how you aim to act along the way.

Your strategy should consider the following, many of which you'll have identified already from your preparation in Step 1:

- **What you want to have:** These should include your 'must-haves' and a few 'give-aways' that you can offer if necessary.

- **What you must have:** These are your minimum requirements. You need these for the negotiation to be successful.

- **Your BATNA:** This is your Best Alternative To a Negotiated Agreement. If you simply can't get what you want, your BATNA is your second-best option.

- **Your 'walk-away' point:** This is the point where you have to stop negotiating, before you come away with less than your minimum requirements.

- **Your proposed approach:** This is the manner in which you aim to reach a deal. In most cases, bargaining will be the mainstay of your negotiations, but you may find that haggling gets results for specific elements.

Make your strategy watertight

For your strategy to be in with a fighting chance it must be both realistic and informed. To knock it into shape, you can't think about your negotiation strategy in isolation, but must understand the context in which you'll use it.

Am I in the right ballpark?

To create a realistic negotiation proposal, find out as much as you can about the goal that you seek. Say, for example, you're applying for a new job with prospects, but whose salary is just too low for you to start on, and you plan to negotiate it up if you get it. To create a workable strategy, first find out what your own 'market value' is, to avoid setting your sights too low or too high. You might check comparable positions on recruitment websites or in newspaper jobs pages, or speak to an adviser (at a job centre or a recruitment agency) for indicative salaries. Talk to (trusted) contacts who've negotiated pay to understand how their negotiated rise compared against what they'd hoped. If you're representing a supplier company, the same applies; you must find out about your competitors' prices before you set down your own in a negotiation strategy.

Who has the most leverage?

In negotiations 'leverage' is the term used to describe how much weight one party has in influencing how negotiations will turn out. Identifying how much leverage each party has will help you use your negotiation strategy effectively, and this discovery can be surprising. If you're negotiating with a superior e.g. your boss, or a big corporate like your broadband provider, it's easy to assume that they'll have the most leverage, because they're 'higher up' or 'bigger' than you, but this isn't always the case.

Say you've interviewed for a new job and been offered it, though you still enjoy your present job. You could, at this point, meet with your current boss to negotiate better pay, and be the party with the most leverage. Why? You can go into negotiations knowing that you've nothing to lose and everything to gain. If your boss cannot meet your 'must-have' requirements, then you're in the lucky position of your 'walk-away' scenario being exactly that – you can walk into another job. Pulling this information out of the bag when negotiations reach an impasse wields great leverage. Your boss knows that if he/she cannot meet at least your 'must-have' requirements he/she's likely to lose you, and recruitment costs both time and money. Negotiate costs with a big broadband provider that loudly advertises affordability and you, as a paying customer, have some leverage because you've identified better deals, are willing to move elsewhere to get them, and are happy to tell your friends to do so too.

How do I stick to my walk-away points?

The safety-net that lies under your entire strategy is your ability to walk away at any point, before you're drawn by momentum into agreeing on less than your 'must-haves'. Your walk-away points needn't be financially-driven. They can include anything that is unacceptable to you: signing a long contract when you need a shorter one; negotiations that last longer than a specified period; or having to move house if offered a promotion. Be careful to note all your walk-away points. There may be several, and they may be unrelated. They mustn't be decided whilst you're negotiating, but identified in advance, written down in a calm moment, and fixed in stone. They are non-negotiable. Give in on these and you risk everything, including your credibility: in plain terms, you've been walked over – publicly.

How does a BATNA work?

Not every negotiation can arrive at an agreement. Your Best Alternative To a Negotiated Agreement (BATNA) can provide an alternative to walking away and damaging relationships with those you have to work with afterwards. Say you're negotiating with your manager for extra training, but she says 'I simply have no budget for training'. Rather than walk away from the prospect of career progression, your BATNA may provide alternatives to satisfy *some* of your interests. Extra holiday entitlement, or half-day Fridays, would give you some capacity to pursue training under your own steam. The BATNA creatively acknowledges the fact that negotiations have failed to provide agreement now, but that you value the ongoing relationship.

Offer to draw up an agenda

Contact your opposite number, and ask what they'd like on the agenda for discussion. This will reveal the issues that are important to them, possible areas for mutual agreement, and will also highlight those questions that you've not yet considered in your research. Distributing this agenda will tell the opposite party what's important to you, and oblige them to talk about it; they can't wriggle out of an agenda point if they've agreed the document. An agenda saves time and minimizes surprises: no properly structured meeting should wander much from its original format. An advance agenda also removes the fear of the unknown, and gives you a chance to rehearse what you want to say.

Business writing: agendas

This simple but invaluable written document should include the date, time and venue, followed by a list of the people attending. Items for discussion are listed in the order you propose they be discussed, numbered accordingly. If anyone has a specific role, that's worthwhile recording.

Date/Time: 01 February 2014 12:00 p.m. to 2:00 p.m.
Venue: Meeting Room C, Taylor Building
Attendees: Marc Fisher, Sarah Tait, Jim Morton

Items for discussion

1 Marc Fisher's current roles and responsibilities
2 Office changes: next 12 months
3 Changes to office administration roles
4 Possible extra responsibilities for key staff
5 Training requirements

RESPONSIBILITIES

Record meeting decisions: Jim Morton

Make an educated guess about their strategy

By undertaking preparatory research about your opposite number, you may have an idea about what their negotiation strategy will be. An advance agenda will definitely clarify things further. But if, despite having done your homework, you still feel you don't know what to expect, it's still worthwhile making an educated guess, or guesses. Asking yourself the following questions will help you explore possible scenarios in your head. It may help you form an idea of the opposite party's likely strategy and also whip your own into shape:

■ Are they likely to open with a proposal?

■ What might their proposals be?

■ What arguments do I have to counter them?

■ Do I think they will be 'tough' or accommodating?

■ How are they going to respond to my must-haves?

■ What counters will they have to my proposals?

■ Do I think they will give me a 'take it or leave it' ultimatum?

■ How will they rate the importance of my USP?

Asking yourself such simple, open questions will start you thinking creatively about how to respond to any number of scenarios. 'Dealing with' something in your head in advance of the meeting will make the real thing less surprising, and much less daunting.

Road test your strategy

If you're feeling nervous about negotiating, be assured that you're not alone. Like learning any difficult new skill, practice can both minimize anxiety and improve your performance.

Ask a friend to play a tough-nut negotiator over coffee one weekend, and try out your negotiation strategy against your educated guess at your opponent's. Roleplay will not only help you practise speaking persuasively about your 'must-haves', but will sharpen your ability to think on your feet – vital in negotiations. Note those moments that you found particularly hard to get through: do you tend to lose your train of thought if someone interrupts you? Do you get upset if someone dismisses your argument? Identifying pressure points and finding ways to deal with them before you really have to is invaluable. Ask your friend for feedback – were your arguments compelling? Did you sell yourself? How confident was your body language? Their answers could be revealing.

Choose your venue

Just like in football, it's usually preferable to negotiate on 'home turf', where you feel most secure. However, the importance of this can get over-emphasized, so don't fret if you fail to persuade the other party to yours. Negotiating on their patch may not be your first choice but there are perks: because you're an invited guest, you don't need to deal with the details of providing hospitality, and can concentrate on the negotiations, and nothing else.

Meeting in a neutral location such as a hired meeting room or over coffee is just as good, potentially better. Not only are you both on an equal footing, but finding your feet somewhere new can offer opportunities for breaking the ice before you start: finding power points and water coolers becomes a group activity, gets both sides talking and helps you relax.

If talks are on home turf, avoid out-dated power games like sitting in an upholstered chair while the opposite party squirms on plastic ones. Try sitting round a table or side by side, rather than across it, to make both sides feel this is a shared problem rather than a head-to-head. Provide breaks, good refreshments, and make sure everyone knows where the restrooms are.

Your self-preparation

You've spent valuable time gathering information ahead of your negotiations, now it's time to gather yourself too. Sparing a thought for your physical presentation is not a wasted effort; going into negotiation feeling good about yourself not only improves your own confidence; it will send out strong positive messages to those you are about to negotiate with too.

Dress

It won't come as a surprise to hear that when approaching the negotiations table, you should look your best. Wearing business clothes that make you feel and look both professional and purposeful, will help boost your self-confidence and suggest to the other party that you are not someone to be walked over. Here are a few points to bear in mind:

■ **Don't overdress:** avoid wearing brand new clothes that have obviously been bought specially, or you may appear a bit desperate – suggesting to others that underneath the smart togs you're lacking in confidence. Similarly, don't wear clothes that make you fiddle or tweak; frequent readjustment of clothing can reveal underlying nerves, giving the other party a confidence advantage, and distracting you at a time when you should be paying close attention to every word that's being uttered.

- **Be comfortable:** you've no doubt heard it before but it's worth repeating: avoid wearing uncomfortable clothes no matter how great you look in them. People who are feeling pinched or prickled by their clothes look visibly ill at ease, appear less confident, and usually don't feel great either. For your negotiations, wear something you've worn several times before, but that you invariably feel good in. Then you can forget what you're wearing and get on with the job of negotiating.

- **Be presentable:** if you have had to travel some way to negotiations, don't let it show. No matter the time or how early a start you made, you must never look dishevelled, even if you did drive for four hours to be there. Everything you wear should be spotless, pressed and fresh. When planning travel, choose clothes that don't crease easily, so that you can arrive looking clean-cut and ready for anything.

Timeliness

Arrive in good time for negotiations. Lateness can be mis-construed in a number of ways: that you don't care about the outcome; that you're (foolishly) playing mind-games with the opposite party; or that you're just plain unprofessional. Any of these can wreak havoc with what could have been a level playing field: others may interpret lateness as disorganization, a weakness they can exploit by playing 'hard', or they may interpret lateness as a power trip that encourages an equally aggressive response. Whatever the interpretation, arriving late won't allow you time to acclimatize to your surroundings, unpack your materials, and gather your thoughts. Think back to the last time you were late for an important appointment – the anxiety of being late tends to hang around you, and anxiety is one emotion you really don't want to reveal too readily when negotiating.

Arriving early can, in fact, be very helpful, especially if you're entering into team negotiations. If you're on their patch, being early lets you get to grips with your surroundings – like where the water-cooler and restrooms are, getting you onto a level playing field with them. Arriving early allows you speak to people before they take their seats, put names to faces, and engage in small talk (using your previous research as a jumping off point). It's easier to be tough on strangers than friends: having time to share just one common interest with a member of the other party makes it harder for everyone to be aggressive during negotiations.

Your entrance and attitude

Research suggests that over 50 per cent of communication is non-verbal, and that people form a first (and lasting) impression of you within ten seconds. That being the case, even the manner in which you walk into your negotiation meeting will affect how the other party estimates your potential leverage against their own.

Walk in with purpose, with your head up and looking attentive. Do your best to look happy to be there, even though your stomach may feel like mush. Facing the meeting with a bright face, a smile, and a positive demeanour will tell others (and your team if you have one) that you're quietly confident, and will also reassure everyone that you are an optimist who is ready to find a creative and mutually beneficial solution. Positivity is infectious; you can, to an extent, make the whole process a little more pleasant by going in with the right appearance and frame of mind, because it eases everyone's jitters and makes them less likely to be aggressive.

Walk into negotiations with a daunted look, and you'll paint yourself as a victim, essentially inviting the other party to use you as a doormat. Even if they do try to be reasonable, if they see that you are openly terrified, it's unlikely that they will propose any creative solutions that would require two-way bargaining and longer talks. By being kind and keeping things short, they will effectively present you with their solution, not a negotiated one. Either way, you lose.

Refine your body language for the negotiating table

A handshake speaks volumes

Before you take your seat at any negotiating table you should shake hands with each member of the opposite party, even if that's just your boss. A firm handshake will underline that you are purposeful, confident, and committed to agreement. Offer a limp handshake and you'll suggest that you're either negotiating reluctantly or are plain terrified, neither of which you want to communicate to the other party.

Make eye contact and smile

Meeting the eyes of the opposite party will be a powerful moment, which can communicate exactly how you're feeling. So, in the days preceding, become aware of how you use eye contact. No matter how nervous you are, you should aim to convey that you're happy to be there – almost excited to get started. Eye contact builds trust, makes a great first impression, and communicates equality – we use the phrase 'he wouldn't look me in the eye' to describe someone who is frightened, ashamed or deferring in some way – so be ready to look 'em in the eye.

Resist your nervous tics

All of us have them – those annoying habits that appear when we're feeling uptight. Whether it's talking through your fingers or rubbing your nose, ask a trusted friend to help you pinpoint your tics before you negotiate, and learn to resist them. At best, such habits underline your anxiety. At worst, some believe that nervous tics accompany lying. Whether that's a valid observation or not, don't give others any cause for doubt.

Sustaining positive body language

Your negotiation meeting or series of meetings may be quite lengthy, and it's important to convey consistently positive body language throughout, no matter how wearing the process is. Before negotiations, try to become aware of the following aspects of your body language:

- **Your posture:** It's important that you sit upright and look attentive for the duration of your meeting, even though it may be long. Resist the temptation to rest your chin in your upturned palm as it can suggest you're tired or uninterested. Instead, rest your chin on your knuckles, with your fist lightly closed and your elbow propped on the table. This slight change can, contrastingly, suggest concentration and thought.

- **Your emotion indicators:** Beware the signals you are unconsciously sending out; they may give the other party valuable insight into how assured (or not) you are feeling. While a sudden folding of your arms suggests you disagree or are angry, excessive blinking or rubbing your eyes and face suggests you feel overwhelmed or defeated – it's no coincidence that gamblers have 'poker-faces'. Keep your feet still too, especially if they are visible. Just because they are below eye level doesn't mean they won't tell tales.

- **Your head carriage:** We lower our heads when we feel browbeaten or put upon. Raising your head expresses assurance, and if you need it, even defiance. Resist all temptation to lower your head, as it may admit defeat. Turn your head and look into the eyes of every person who speaks: it conveys engagement, interest, energy and equality.

Consider your voice

However misplaced it may be, people make assumptions about us and what we have to say judged simply on the way we speak. This can work both for and against us, especially in negotiations. If you use it well, your voice (backed up by confident body language) can be an incredibly persuasive instrument, actively helping you to get what you want. Before negotiating, it's therefore a worthwhile exercise to consider just how you come across to other people when you speak. To ensure you're making the most of your voice and delivery, ask yourself the following questions:

■ Do you fall over your words when you talk about something important?

■ Do others often ask you to speak up or repeat yourself?

■ Do others often ignore you?

■ Do other people turn round to glance at you when you first speak?

■ Do others sometimes physically step back from you when you speak?

If you find that you are answering 'yes' to any of the questions above, it may be the right time to consider your voice and how you use it. In the days preceding negotiation, make a concerted effort to listen to yourself speaking to colleagues and family, and be aware of how they respond to your voice.

A common characteristic of the best negotiators is that they are compelling and deliberate speakers. Making positive adjustments to your own voice and delivery could not only boost your self-confidence ahead of negotiations, but help you at work and off-duty too.

Pace

Do you fall over your words and get breathless when you speak? If so, it's likely you're speaking too fast. In negotiations, you want the opposite party to hear, and digest, everything you say, so it's up to you to deliver that information clearly. In addition, speaking too fast not only reveals nerves, but can worsen them too, both of which are worth avoiding during negotiations. If you do tend to stumble over your words when discussing important things, note the points from your negotiation-strategy 'road test' where you became emotional or anxious. Repeatedly practising what you want to say at these points will eventually take the emotion out of it, until you can say what you want to, clearly and calmly.

Volume

If other people constantly ask you to repeat yourself, or worse, ignore you, it's time to speak up. In negotiations an overly-quiet voice can suggest lack of conviction in what you've got to say, or lack of self-confidence, either of which can leave you vulnerable. At the other end of the spectrum – if others glance your way when you first speak or take an involuntary step back if you join a conversation, it's time to turn down your volume. Talking too loudly in negotiations could be construed as misplaced confidence or aggression. Whatever your issue, practise before you negotiate; at home, read aloud to a friend or family member, controlling your volume until they hear everything, comfortably. Ask others for honest feedback, and act on it.

Your online and office persona

You've done your research, you've prepared your strategy and you're thinking about your body language and voice. Now it's time to think about how others – especially your opposite number – estimate you based on the information that's readily available to them from a number of sources, not least the Internet.

LinkedIn®

Before negotiations, ensure your profile is accurate and up to date. Ask trusted contacts if they'd be willing to endorse your skills or write you a recommendation. If you're negotiating for something specific with your boss, e.g. training in a new skill, you could tweak your profile to display ambition in this area. If your opposite number takes the time to check your profile, this could make your negotiations case all the more compelling.

Facebook

Be careful what you post and who sees it. If you don't want the other party seeing your private life, ensure access to your photos is limited to friends only. Ensure your profile picture (visible even when your account is private) isn't one that will compromise your chances of promotion! The same goes for Twitter and all the other social networking sites. Lock them down so that you have to approve followers, or post carefully. Preferably both.

In the office

If you're planning negotiations with your boss or a colleague, now is the time to become an exemplary office member. In the weeks preceding, (and if you are not already) be punctual, be accommodating, be fair, be professional and presentable. Again, if you're negotiating to gain something specific, make sure your behaviour emphasizes those abilities or commitment to that idea. If you're negotiating, say, for flexible working, be careful to display good time management and punctuality, and don't talk too much about your demanding kids or home life – you must try to embody the idea that what you want may actually be right for everybody, not just yourself. If you're hoping to negotiate promotion, consider ways to display your capacity for extra responsibility, such as learning to use a new software package in the office, or even asking a colleague to help you gain a new skill.

Key take-aways

Write down the things you will take away from Step 2 and how you will implement them.

Topic	Take-away	Implementation
How to create your negotiation strategy	• Identify 'must-haves' and 'want-to-haves'. • Identify walk away points, BATNA and deal approach.	• Think about what I must 'get' to consider my negotiations a success. • Consider what I can do if I have to walk away.
How to research your strategy's context to make it realistic and informed		
How to make an informed guess about your opposite number's negotiation strategy		
Understanding leverage and how to maximize it		
How to fix walk-away points and stick to them		
Understanding and identifying a BATNA		
How to make the most of any negotiations venue		
How to prepare physically for negotiating		
How to check and improve your office and online persona ahead of a negotiation		

Step 3

TAKE CONTROL IN THE EARLY STAGES

'The aim of argument, or of discussion, should not be victory, but progress.'
— Joseph Joubert, (1754–1824),
French essayist and moralist

Five ways to succeed

- Learn to identify which negotiation stage you're in.
- Be full and honest about your objectives.
- Listen carefully to the opposite party.
- Increasingly refine your questions to gain information.
- Think of the negotiation as a shared problem.

Five ways to fail

- Ensure negotiations stick strictly to the five stages.
- Never waste time discussing the procedure of the negotiation.
- Plan what you want to say while the other party speaks.
- Always explain your interests before the other party does.
- Use technical terms to confuse the other party.

The different stages of negotiation

When you're negotiating, it's crucial to have a shared understanding of what point you're at in the negotiations. Expensive mistakes can be made if one party in the negotiations thinks they're outlining their needs and the other party thinks they're reaching a final agreement.

To help 'place' yourself within negotiation, as well as organize everything you want to share, ask for, and achieve, it's helpful to think of negotiations as a five-stage process. Understanding the five stages of negotiation will not only help you organize your own mind, but will help you understand the other party's position and pace, and where they are in the negotiation.

■ **Stage 1: Explain**
Each side explains their needs, and describes what they expect from the negotiation.

■ **Stage 2: Explore**
Each party discusses the other's situation, asking questions to find out more about what the other expects.

■ **Stage 3: Propose**
One or both sides make initial proposals.

■ **Stage 4: Bargain**
Both parties bargain about what they can offer, asking the other party for concessions to try to agree on terms.

■ **Stage 5: Agree**
This is the stage you all want to get to; a 'buying signal' tells you the other party is ready to agree.

Sounding Pro

It's helpful to consider what each stage sounds like in reality, so that when you hear key words you can orientate yourself within the negotiation. Here are some examples of the kind of language you might hear at each stage.

Stage 1: Explain *The way I see things, there is a definite need for an office management role.*

The problem I have is how to work more shifts but still be as productive.

What I want to achieve is to improve my performance with relevant training.

Stage 2: Explore *Tell me what you think an office manager's responsibilities could be.*

What kind of training do you think would have most impact on my/your performance?

Stage 3: Propose *I propose we do this.*

How would you feel if I were to offer you more hours?

I suggest we speak to HR about possible flexible working patterns.

Stage 4: Bargain *If we create an office manager role for you, will you work full-time?*

If you agree to increased, but flexible, hours, I'm ready to draw up a contract.

If you can't agree to this training, I'll have to withdraw the offer of funding.

Stage 5: Agree *I'm happy with that. / I can live with that. Let's proceed on those lines. / Let's just agree that then.*

Of course, negotiations will rarely follow the five-stage process exactly, because that's not how people work; we change our minds and have new ideas. When you're negotiating, for example, someone may add new information, with the result that negotiations jump from the Bargaining Stage back into the Explain or Explore Stages, where new ideas get road-tested fully. In negotiation, the trick isn't to pedantically 'impose' the five-part process, but to be able to identify and navigate them – as disordered as they may be – to mutual benefit.

By being able to identify each stage in a negotiation you will always have a roadmap of what is expected of you at any given point, so, for example, you won't make yourself look naive by wading into bargaining before anyone has even explored the issues in hand. Perhaps even more crucially, having an understanding of the stages will make it easier for you to spot if you're being hurried into an agreement or stalled by delays, giving you the ability to take control of negotiations that aren't progressing in a way that you find acceptable. Regaining the helm like this is a skill in itself, and one which we will examine in detail in Step 6.

By this time you may have undertaken considerable preparation for your approaching negotiation. The first two phases of negotiation – the Explain and Explore phases – could be considered an extension of that preparation, but contrastingly, are undertaken as a joint venture, at the negotiating table, *with* your opposite party.

The Explain Stage

The purpose of the Explain Stage

At the Explain Stage of negotiation, you will present your interests in the negotiation based on your negotiation strategy, which has already identified the following:

1 What you want to achieve: including must-haves and a few give-aways

2 What you must have: your minimum requirements for a successful negotiation

3 Your BATNA: your second-best option if you can't reach a negotiated agreement

4 Your walk-away point: the point where you must stop negotiating before you lose out

With these firmly in mind, you and the opposite party should do three things at the Explain Stage:

1 **Agree the procedures of the negotiation,** e.g. what's on the agenda, how much time you have, how you'll record what's agreed, how often you'll break etc.

2 **Explain your objectives,** e.g. to secure improved terms and conditions in a contract etc.

3 **Explain your situation and the opportunities for mutual benefit that you see,** e.g. you might mention your capacity for increased responsibility, or how a fixed 9–5 working day is compromising your effectiveness.

This 'scene-setting' stage allows everyone to talk freely, identify coinciding objectives, and establish the beginnings of rapport and trust.

Agreeing procedures

In negotiations, especially complex ones, it's important to briefly discuss how both parties see negotiations 'going', so that you don't get any surprises along the way. Here are some examples of the kind of thing to agree before proceeding:

■ Is everyone happy with what's on the agenda?

■ Are there going to be any presentations? If so, how long will they take?

■ When are you scheduling comfort breaks? If it's an all-day meeting, when and where is lunch, and who is providing it?

■ Is it okay to interrupt each other, even during a presentation, to ask clarifying questions, or should questions be held until the person has finished?

■ Is it okay to ask for a break, e.g. if you're negotiating with a team and need to talk?

■ Do you both expect to complete negotiations today, or do you expect to negotiate further by phone or email?

■ Do you have to be out of the room by a certain time?

■ Who is recording decisions made?

■ Do both parties have authority to conclude an agreement?

Discussing these apparently minor details is not time wasted; it is an investment in the smooth running of the meeting that saves everyone both time and effort.

Being clear about your objectives

It's important in the Explain Stage to be honest about what you want to achieve. This, in plain terms, is your 'What I want to have' from your negotiation strategy. There is no point in saying that you want one thing now, and, once you've gained confidence, adding a long wish-list later on – that will only force both parties back to the Explain and Explore Stages all over again so that they can clarify what your interests really are. Holding information back could cause delays and irritate the other party, which may compromise chances of agreement. Instead, be truthful and clear about what it is you hope to achieve in general terms. Don't make any demands, don't get bogged down in detail (that will come later), and don't be defensive. Just explain what you want: be open, be optimistic, and be succinct. This isn't the time for a long monologue.

Sharing information

Now is the time for both parties to begin amicably sharing information on each other's true interests and objectives, and presenting any information which is pertinent to the whole negotiation.

- **Explain the background:** What has brought you to your decision to meet today? How is your current situation unsatisfactory – and maybe not just for you? Perhaps it's impacting on your effectiveness, and is affecting your colleagues too?

- **Present helpful and relevant information:** Use your preparatory research to gain some leverage. Say you're negotiating for a pay-rise, for example; now would be the time to share your findings about the current 'market value' of positions comparable to yours. If you're hoping to secure flexible working, you could share statistics you've found on the improved productivity of flexible workers.

- **Share deadlines for delivery of the agreement:** This may lead to the sharing of timing-driven 'walk-away' points too, giving everyone a strong motivation for successful completion. Deadlines can be positive motivators: perhaps, if you're hoping to secure funded training, you may explain that fees will go up in the next academic year, for example.

- **Explain your objectives in the context of a potentially mutual benefit:** Always try to see how your needs can complement those of the other party, e.g. 'if you fund me now, you'll get the training more cheaply' or 'if you can offer me flexible hours, I'll be able to work more effectively', and so on. Emphasizing causal links like these could be pivotal in your negotiations.

The Explore Stage

This is a creative, two-way stage, where both sides will share and discover lots of information they may not yet have appreciated. You and your opposite party should do three main things in the Explore Stage:

- **Ask each other questions:** e.g. 'Could you tell me a bit more about your current working patterns?'

- **Ask for clarification of things you don't yet understand:** e.g. 'Are you convinced that only a move to flexible working will provide you with the balance you need?'

- **Check that you have understood your opposite party's position or interests correctly:** e.g. 'So, would I be right in saying that you'd actually like to take on more hours – if you could work them flexibly?'

This fact-finding exercise provides both sides with options to concede or trade for a mutually beneficial agreement. You may get asked a lot of questions: don't assume you're being interrogated or get defensive. Lots of questions indicate how interested both parties are in reaching agreement. But keep your negotiation strategy in mind at all times. If you (or your team) have decided not to divulge some information, don't let this conversational stage distract you into sharing it unthinkingly.

The key elements of the Explore Stage

The usefulness of the Explore Stage hangs on two key elements: being willing to actively listen, and building trust. By happy coincidence, however, these two go hand in hand. Listening actively (within which asking questions is a vital element), then repeating back what you think you have heard, or summarizing how you think the other side is feeling, are all processes that we undertake to gain – and maintain – the trust of others. These processes are very similar to those that we see when we share a problem with a friend, for example; he or she may not offer us a solution, but they explore our situation, listen intently, and echo back what they think the problem is or how they think we feel. The sharer feels unburdened, and both people enjoy a renewed sense of trust. This is the aim of the Explore Stage – not only are both parties trying to uncover every possible option for agreement, but at the same time are trying to understand each other and establish a relationship. The agenda is briefly on hold, resentments are shelved for a moment, and the discussion is (ideally) amicable and understanding, instilling a sense of mutual trust which will serve both sides well on what may be a tense road ahead.

Active listening in negotiations

In negotiations, being able to listen well offers you a number of advantages: it helps you to gain the trust of the opposite party, it displays your commitment to negotiations and your willingness to be reasonable, and it allows you to glean important information about the other party's needs – both what they openly declare, and what you can interpret from what they say at other times. It's worthwhile spending some time identifying what kind of a listener you currently are, and making every effort to improve your listening skills before approaching the negotiating table.

The four types of listeners

Research has identified four types of listener:

Non listeners

Non listeners are more interested in what they have to say themselves than in the person they're talking to. They hog conversations, and fill in the natural gaps in their own monologue using long 'ums' and 'ems' to prevent others speaking. They will actively talk over others who attempt to interject, and talk over other people's 'verbal nods' such as 'really?' and 'oh, I see', in order to push a point. They'll leave conversations having remembered little that other people managed to say, and will invariably have the last word.

Marginal listeners

Marginal listeners are also more interested in what they have to say themselves than the person they're talking to. In negotiations, they may often interrupt so that they can tell others what they're thinking, or use what the other person says as an introduction to what they want to say. Often impatient, they will finish other people's sentences, check back over their notes while others talk, tap their pens or fingers, and are easily distracted by things going on around them.

Pretend listeners

Pretend listeners appear to listen but are actually observing other people's characters and judging what they say. As they listen, they're deciding how to respond, so they're planning, rather than listening. They're not concerned with how others feel; they 'hear the words' but they 'don't hear the feelings'. In negotiations they'll get all the facts of the situation, but may not consider the emotions involved.

Active listeners

Active listeners are quiet and sympathetic. They listen to what others say, and pay attention to how they feel by trying to put themselves in their shoes. They encourage people to fully express themselves and to continue speaking. They don't interrupt. They wait for others to finish before they respond. They ask meaningful questions to encourage the speaker onwards without derailing them. Active listeners make confident, engaged eye contact, quiet 'verbal nods' like 'I see ...' and will support the speaker with facial expressions that underpin key points in the conversation. They'll appear quite 'still', and may lean forward a little to listen. They notice verbal and visual cues that tell them someone wants to speak, and will 'give them the floor' if it's appropriate, often with a deferring hand gesture. Active listeners respect privacy, personal space, and spot physical barriers – they make take off their specs, or remove small obstacles between themselves and the speaker.

The truth is we're probably all four types of listener at different times, depending on the conversation, how we feel, and who we're with. But it's clear that becoming an active listener will serve you best in a negotiations context. People who listen well gain the trust of others far more quickly than poor listeners. Listening fully to others also makes other people feel valued. Put together, being a good listener helps others think of you as trustworthy, genuine, and interested, all of which are characteristics that could maximize your chances of negotiation success.

Become an active listener using FACE

Some people, albeit few, are 'born listeners'. For the rest of us, there's a useful technique called FACE, which stands for:

- **Focus:** Focus on the speaker and on nothing else. Focus not only on what they say but also how they feel. Try to appreciate the full experience of the communication without judging. Verbal nods like 'Hm' or 'Uh huh' reassure the speaker that you're fully focused on them.

- **Acknowledge:** Acknowledge both a person's desire to speak and that 'they have the floor'. Tilt your head to show that you're listening, or assume facial expressions that mirror the tone of the subject under discussion. Unobtrusive expressions like 'I see', 'I understand', show that you're paying attention.

- **Clarify:** Ask simple, meaningful questions to encourage the speaker. Open questions encourage fuller responses: 'What are your career priorities?' Targeted questions get straight answers: 'How quickly could you go full-time?'

- **Empathize:** Show that you appreciate the speaker's opinion or experience. Empathize not only through what you say, (e.g. 'I understand you're worried about that.') but also by the tone and volume of your voice, your attentive body language and facial expressions.

Using FACE will not only help you establish mutual trust in the Explore Stage, but help you gain valuable information too.

Making active listening work for you

It's a simple fact of negotiations that the person with the most information is likely to gain a better outcome – possibly for both parties. They will be able to offer creative solutions that haven't been thought of, or be aware of underlying interests that no one else has addressed. The quickest route to gaining information in the Explore Stage is to speak less and listen more. Here's how:

■ **Let the other person speak first:** It's not always possible, but their speaking first can focus both your listening and questioning. If your boss has briefly mentioned that he's interested in pushing the company's social media presence, you'll realize that selling your spreadsheet abilities as a USP may be time wasted, but that you could helpfully redirect your questions onto social media training, for example.

■ **Listen to their vocabulary:** Note when others use phrases like 'I need' versus 'I want' or 'I would like'. Such choices reveal what's truly important to them, and what their walkaway points may be. Be aware also if these word choices are unstable – do they swap them around in an unguarded moment? This may imply that they're unsure what they need, or expect to gain less than they say, both of which may provide you with some leverage. If your boss says he 'needs' you to work weekend shifts, then later says he 'would like' you to work weekend shifts, it's clear he's not confident that you will agree to them, nor that he can force you.

■ **Increasingly refine your questions:** Begin with open-ended questions that encourage a full response, then refine your questions from there. So, for example, you may begin by asking questions like 'Can you tell me about what you need from my team?' which would reveal many of the other party's 'want to haves', into which you can drill down into specifics e.g. 'So, I understand that you need delivery by 4th August; can I ask why this date specifically?' Getting to the heart of *why* people want things – how, and when – can provide valuable material for concession, compromise or a creative alternative (remember your BATNA).

■ **Listen for the things they're not saying:** In the Explore phrases, both parties may say many things, but are there areas that the opposite party slithers around carefully, or are they non-committal on some areas that you want to know more about? Be aware of one party deliberately avoiding certain topics; it's likely that these are the very areas you should know more about. You may have to proceed with tact, asking politely probing questions like 'I sense you're a little reluctant to talk about this; would it be okay to ask if there is anything I should be concerned about?'

■ **Don't hurry to fill a gap:** Nobody likes an awkward silence, and most people will do anything to fill it. In negotiations, leave an occasional pause and continue to listen; the other party may tack on an additional piece of information just to fill the gap.

Your vocabulary and attitude

The Explore Stage is the last preparatory stage of negotiations before you move into the active stages of Proposing, Bargaining and Agreeing. The impression you give in the Explore Stage will shape the way the opposite party works with you in the following stages, so be mindful of your attitude to the negotiation, and the vocabulary you use to reflect that attitude.

Mind your language

In negotiations, perhaps more than at any other time, you want every word to work for you, rather than against you. Here are a few pointers to make every word count:

- **Don't exaggerate:** Exaggeration makes it difficult for the other party to pinpoint what your real interests are, which can be counter-productive. Say, for example, you're negotiating with your boss for a better office space. Saying that your position in the office, next to the vending machine is 'driving you insane' doesn't tell her much. However, explaining that the background noise in the area, and the distraction of people chatting there 'makes it difficult to concentrate' or is 'making it hard to hit my deadlines' gets straight to the heart of the issue, and gives her a clear motivation to sort it out.

■ **Avoid words underlining inability:** When you're being asked about your situation in the Explore Stage, make a conscious effort not to overuse words like 'can't', 'don't' or 'won't', which can make you appear unmotivated to strive for a beneficial agreement. Of course you'll have to use some negative vocabulary, but try to counterbalance it with positive language that describes an imagined solution, e.g. 'I just can't work as effectively as I'd like right now, but I *can* see how different things would be if I could work flexibly'. This not only voices your commitment to finding a mutual solution, but paints an attractive picture of how things could work.

■ **Avoid insistent interrogation:** The Explore Stage is all about getting to the heart of the matter. But try to avoid being too insistent, especially if emotions are running high. Over-use of the word 'why' can be harshly direct, and if repeatedly used, can make others feel like they're being interrogated. Not every question need begin with 'why', so ensure that your questions are varied and appropriate to the discussion. Although it perhaps shouldn't be the case, your superiors may also resent it if you use the word 'why' to challenge them directly, which could work against you.

■ **Avoid jargon:** You will not gain leverage by using obscure acronyms or business jargon to come across more informed than the other party. This kind of mind-game is long out-dated. You're more likely to look a bit insecure, or worse, a bit of an idiot.

Work on your attitude

Negotiations are more likely to reach a mutually beneficial solution if the parties involved go in with a positive attitude. Central to this is thinking about the negotiation not as having two opposing sides, but as one shared problem being resolved by two parties in partnership. This may sound a bit unrealistic, but by simply using the language of shared responsibility you're not only more likely to get a positive response from the opposite party, it will also help you be objective about your situation. To do this, attempt to avoid language that takes sides, such as 'you' versus 'me': 'you've made it impossible for me to progress'. This sounds accusing and aggressive. Try couching the problem in terms that don't apportion blame, e.g. 'I've found it increasingly difficult to progress at work'. Allow the other party to draw out the reasons, rather than you verbally pointing the finger first.

Key take-aways

Write down the things you will away take from Step 3 and how you will implement them.

Topic	Take-away	Implementation
How to recognize which stage of the negotiation you are in	• *Listen out for key 'pointer' phrases like 'I suggest we do this.'*	• *Note what these stages feel like when I'm negotiating day to day e.g. with my kids.*
How to conduct the Explain Stage of negotiation successfully		
How to conduct the Explore Stage of negotiation successfully		
How to identify the different types of listener		
How to become an active listener		
How to make active listening work in negotiations		
How to use positive vocabulary to underpin a positive attitude		

Step 4

PROPOSE, BARGAIN AND AGREE

'Here's the rule for bargains. "Do other men, for they would do you." That's the true business precept.'
— Charles Dickens (1812–1870):
Martin Chuzzlewit

Five ways to succeed

- Emphasize the shared benefits of your proposals.
- Rehearse your initial proposal for maximum persuasiveness.
- Let the other party open if you're unsure how high to pitch.
- Don't let bargaining make you forget your walk-away points.
- Always confirm what you have agreed on as you go.

Five ways to fail

- Never divulge how a proposal could benefit you.
- Never be stuck for words – always have an answer.
- If a proposal makes you angry, show it.
- Haggle early in negotiations to show confidence.
- In bargaining emails, don't waste time on social niceties.

The Propose Stage

You and your opposite number have now explained your situations, and spent time sharing information in the Explain and Explore Stages. Now it's time to shift up a gear, into the active stages of negotiation, where we'll learn about making and responding to proposals, bargaining, and reaching agreement. For many, these are the most nerve-wracking stages of negotiation, but if you've prepared thoroughly, and remained objective through the Explain and Explore Stages, there's little to fear. Because of what you have discovered about each other in the Explain and Explore Stages, you and the opposite party should now be working from a relatively solid foundation of mutual understanding, with a degree of rapport that will help in the next stages.

The Propose Stage sequence

When you propose, you make an offer to the other negotiator, which opens up a dialogue that should loosely follow these rules, in this order:

- **Rule 1:** Make your initial proposals on the basis of what you identified in the Explore Stage.

- **Rule 2:** Allow the other side to make counter proposals.

- **Rule 3:** Sell the benefits of the proposal to the other side.

- **Rule 4:** Explain the benefits of the proposal for you.

Sounding Pro

So, on the basis of these four rules, here are some general examples of how you might successfully counter and contribute in the Propose Stage:

1 Making a proposal	*I suggest we undertake a three-month trial of flexible working.*
	I propose that I should be put forward for a company car allowance.
2 Inviting counter-proposals	*How would you respond to this?*
	What do you think of this proposal?
	How do you feel about this?
3 Selling the benefits to the other party	*This will mean I will be able to take on more hours.*
	This will mean I'll be able to take on greater responsibility and train other staff too.
	With a company car I'll have greater reach and be able to increase your customer base.
4 Explaining the benefits to you	*I'll be able to work flexibly and organize my family life around work better.*
	With extra training I'll feel more fulfilled and have better hopes of advancement within the company.
	I'll feel more confident arriving at clients, and a company car is a real incentive for me to stick with the company.

Making a proposal

There are arguments for and against making the opening proposal, so don't worry if your hand is forced on the day. There are advantages to either scenario, so plan for both.

An opening proposal can colour both the mood and the effectiveness of the negotiations to follow. Open harshly and you may set the tone for tetchy negotiations with both sides reluctant to cooperate. Open positively and you may set an atmosphere of interest and understanding whose effects can last right through to agreement. Remember these points when you're formulating an ideal opening proposal:

- Make it clear and enthusiastic, e.g.: 'I'd like to propose a three-month trial of flexible working.'

- Underline the shared benefits, e.g.: 'By being able to balance my family commitments better, my performance in the office will improve.'

- Display confidence in yourself and the proposal too, e.g.: 'I'm convinced of the immediate benefits for both of us.'

- Suggest some degree of flexibility, e.g.: 'We could carry out an appraisal after three months to see how it's going.'

- Create interest in how the proposal would work, e.g.: 'I think it will be easy to put in place and that we'll see a positive impact on the office as a whole.'

You may want to rehearse in the days preceding negotiations, as an assured delivery of your opening proposal can strengthen its persuasiveness and credibility. But remember your proposal is not the end of the negotiation; it's just the first step, so stay on your toes for the counter-proposal.

Pitching your opening proposal

With the previous elements of your proposal in mind, now aim high. If you've effectively explored the reasonable parameters of your interests in the Explain and Explore Stages, your opening proposal is unlikely to come as any surprise to your opposite party – you will have discussed it to some extent already. So do aim high. Make your opening proposal your ideal scenario, your ideal negotiated result. Even if it's unmanageable by the other party, the aspiration level of your opening proposal sets a benchmark for both negotiators to work from in the bargaining stage in order to reach a mutually satisfactory result – it gives both sides wiggle room to work with.

Pitching your opening proposal too low is more dangerous: your opening position will already be precariously close to your walk-away point, giving both parties less material to work with, less chance of a mutually satisfactory result, and a greater risk that you, personally, will seriously lose out.

Be prepared to justify your initial proposal; if you're unable to do this, you may be forced to start making immediate concessions. Respond to objections to your proposal positively by asking questions, rather than making concessions or getting defensive e.g: 'In what ways do you think flexible working could be disruptive?' This allows discussion to continue, despite initial rejection, and allows you to uncover which parts of your proposal are acceptable and which are not. This may allow you to reintroduce your proposal with the emphasis tweaked to attract the other party.

When the other party opens

You needn't think you have lost out because you didn't get to speak first. There are distinct advantages to the other party opening:

■ **If you're not sure how high to pitch your opening proposal:** In this case it can be helpful to let the other party open. This gives you a starting point to work from and has the positive effect of immediately informing your counter response – you won't feel like you're taking a 'shot in the dark'.

■ **If you're nervous about negotiating:** It may help you to allow the other party to open, as it gives you the prompt to reply – a lot less nerve-wracking than speaking up first.

■ **If you think it will work in your favour:** If, for example, you're working with someone who you suspect may immediately make a very good offer, you can encourage them to make an opening proposal as you reach the end of the Explore Stage. Use leading questions such as 'In terms of what we've just discussed, could you make an offer?' or 'What would be your budget for my training?' It takes guts, but it works.

Even if the other party's opening proposal is immediately unacceptable, remember you have all of the negotiation to bring the agreement closer to your own objectives. In the days preceding, loosely planning an imagined sequence of proposals and counter proposals (based on your preparatory research) will reassure you that there is plenty of room for manoeuvre.

Making a counter proposal

So, the other party has opened, and the proposal they've made is less than appealing. What should you do?

■ **Don't fill a gap:** If you're not sure how to counter, saying nothing is better than saying something you may regret later. At best, they may rethink and immediately tweak their proposal. At worst, you've shown them how strongly you feel about their proposal, and displayed your strength of character by not caving.

■ **Don't be affirmative in any way:** Under no circumstances should you say anything that suggests an acceptance of these terms. Be careful even of saying words like 'yes', 'okay' and 'fine' while you digest what you've just heard, or they may (cheekily) run with that as an initial acceptance.

■ **Don't get confrontational:** No matter how shocked or angry you feel, the opening proposal is not the moment to lose your temper. Collect yourself and offer your counter proposal.

■ **Do make your own proposal:** Whatever the opposite party has proposed, you can, of course, just acknowledge it and make your own, planned, initial proposal. So, for example, your boss opens: 'Let's do a three-month trial period of flexible working with you starting from April.' It's January, and you need change now. When your boss says 'How would you feel about that?' you have your cue to present your proposal 'Thanks for that, but I would suggest that full-time, flexible working, would have greater benefits for both of us if I started now.' You've delivered your initial proposal intact and have dangled a perceived benefit. This will trigger your opposite party into asking you what these benefits would be, which may get negotiations rolling.

■ **Do ask questions:** Instead of making concessions, ask questions about their proposal to reveal points where you could reach agreement. Questions like 'How did you arrive at that figure?' or 'Can you explain your plan to delay this until April?' can unearth the motivations for decisions. Understanding these will give both sides more material to trade off in negotiations.

■ **Do ask the other side to help you:** If there is a big gap between their proposal and yours and there seems to be little initial movement, ask for help outright. 'You have proposed this, I have proposed that; how can we bring these two closer?' Such direct questions can reveal surprising insights and creative solutions, distribute responsibility for the problem equally, and concede nothing.

The Bargaining Stage

When you bargain, you discuss options with the other negotiator to find the best solution for both of you. Bargaining is appropriate when maintaining a good relationship after the transaction is important, which is why politicians will predominantly bargain when negotiating with other countries, for example. Bargaining is also best used when there are many parameters – other than just price – to consider, concede or trade off to reach an agreement. You may bargain, for example, when negotiating improved terms and conditions of employment, or when buying services that offer lots of updates and after-care assistance packages to choose from.

The Bargain Stage sequence

Bargaining depends on conditions: 'if you do this, we will do this,' and is most successful when the following rules are considered:

- **Rule 1:** Always make an offer with a condition.

- **Rule 2:** Never give something for nothing.

- **Rule 3:** If you don't like the condition, propose a counter-bargain.

- **Rule 4:** Don't argue, question.

- **Rule 5:** Always confirm what you have agreed before you address issues you *don't* agree on.

And remember: nothing is agreed until everything is agreed – make agreements provisional until the end of the negotiation.

Sounding Pro

So, if you're following these five rules, here are some examples of the language you may both hear and use in the Bargain Stage:

No offer without condition	*If you can agree to flexible working, I can definitely take on full-time hours.*
	If you could manage to hit your sales targets, I could agree to a five per cent pay rise.
	If I fund your training, will you agree to a three-year contract?
Never give something for nothing	*I will offer you the promotion provided you agree to weekend working.*
	I will do this as long as you keep to our agreement.
	I will agree to this provided we can complete within the agreed time frame.
Propose a counter-bargain	*Could I suggest an alternative proposal?*
	Could I suggest we approach this from another angle?
	Let me make a counter-proposal.
Don't argue, question	*Can you explain why you feel that?*
	Please explain to me once more how you arrived at that figure.
	Can you tell me how you reached that decision?
Always confirm agreements	*Let's summarize what we've agreed so far.*
	Let me recap on what we've agreed.
	Before we move on again, let's confirm what we have agreed on.

Bargaining tips

This pacy, interactive stage is fuelled by all of the information that you have uncovered in the Explore Stage. However, successful bargaining relies on both parties not only maintaining adequate momentum, but continuing to listen to each other.

Start positively

When there's a lot to get through, and many issues to settle, it can be very positive to start the Bargain Stage with those issues you're most likely to agree on first. This will raise the morale of both parties and create an element of bargaining rapport.

Stay alert

Bargaining is fuelled by the information revealed in the Explore Stage, which gives you options to trade off in a joint path to agreement. However, be aware of fresh information appearing in the Bargain Stage that further reveals the interests of the other party. Listen carefully to the language used e.g: 'I've had employees abuse flexible working before.' Perhaps you can offer something to allay this fear while securing what you want e.g. 'If you can offer me flexible working, then I'm happy to have an appraisal after three months.' Or you may hear something like 'I'm spending too much on salaries per month as it is.' This initially sounds like a refusal to give you a pay rise, but the question to ask would be 'Is it your fixed costs that are giving you concern?' You may then find out that while a pay rise is unlikely, there may be budget for a bonus scheme or other 'one-off' financial incentive.

Be aware of value

Value isn't all about money. Be aware of what the other party may find valuable that you could trade off easily with little 'cost' to yourself. Say, for example, you run a small catering business and are finding a supplier's costs very high. Would they give you a discount if you offered them discounted rates, or a free hamper of your best new eats? Trading off elements that have perceived value is good for negotiating morale – you just need to identify what you can give away that offers more value to the other than it 'costs' you.

Be aware of pace

The Bargain Stage works best when the pace is brisk and things are getting 'bargained off the to-do list'; the simple sense of 'getting stuff done' helps to keep things positive. However, be aware that this very momentum could make you forget your walk-away points. Don't. Keep them firmly in mind at all times and beware of getting close to them in this cumulative stage. Don't allow yourself to be rushed. If you do feel rushed and don't know how to respond, stop and ask for some time to think – outside the room if necessary.

Keep a record of what's been agreed

As you verbally re-cap what's been agreed, write down these points of agreement at the same time: this minimises scope for argument later. If there's no scribe present, someone, preferably you, must take time out to do this. We'll cover this in more detail in Step 7.

Haggling

While most of your negotiations will rely on the 'give and take' characterized by bargaining, there may be moments *within* the Bargain Stage where you briefly drop into a more simplistic style of negotiation – haggling.

To haggle or not to haggle

Mention haggling and you may imagine tourists quibbling over beach-front souvenirs in the last days of their package holiday. Haggling is what we do when we want to drive down the price of something, or drive up the quantity or quality being offered for the price. This technique works best when what's on offer is a clear-cut item or service that has little scope for adjustment. In most cases, haggling is used when you're less worried about protecting your relationship with the seller after the transaction is completed. However, you may find that you and the other party may briefly drop into haggling to settle very specific or simple points in your negotiations. When haggling takes place as just an isolated element within a wider context of bargaining, it can be effective in settling a simple point quickly – with no damage to the relationship between you and the other party.

While haggling shouldn't be the mainstay of your negotiations, it can have a place when elements of your negotiations are easily quantifiable in terms of number or price: cold, hard figures. Say, for example, your boss has agreed to a promotion, and with it, a car allowance. You may be able to haggle on that figure. Similarly, you could, for example, haggle on notice period too, if you've secured a new job or promotion. You may haggle a quoted notice period up to give you a cushion against redundancy, or haggle it down in order to stay mobile in the job market. Be sensitive to the context though: haggling is pretty informal; it's 'quick and dirty', so it may not be appropriate if your boss or working environment is very formal. Gauge the immediate reaction too: if you get a stunned silence it's unlikely that the other party finds haggling appropriate.

How to haggle

Aim high at the outset

As a premise, haggling relies on one party starting high, the other starting low, and the two meeting in the middle somewhere. So, you would identify what you think would be a great deal and pitch ambitiously for that, in the full knowledge you'd accept something way lower. In response, the other party will knowingly offer their lowest pitch, perhaps saying something like 'That's way out of my league, I'll give you half that.' And so the process continues, each giving a little bit, until you meet somewhere in the middle, with a pretty good deal for both.

Research in advance

Items like annual leave allocation or business mileage expenses may sound perfect candidates for haggling over. However, these may be fixed at company level or higher, so the other party will be genuinely unable to move on these. You must find out ahead of time which figures within your negotiations are genuinely negotiable, and note them as possible haggle points. Try to haggle on a fixed item and you may look like a fool.

Choose your moment

Only drop into haggling if things have gone well and you're 'on the home stretch' towards a full agreement. The other party will be likely to respond more positively if you've already proven your willingness to be fair and make concessions in the interests of a beneficial agreement. Introduce haggling too early while you're still unproven, and you're likely to receive an aggressive or impatient response, which could jeopardize the whole negotiation.

Bargaining by email

Ways of working are becoming more flexible, with companies combining office and home-based workforces. Even small businesses have clients or staff in other countries, with negotiations increasingly carried out on Skype, in conference calls, and by email. While a Skype session or conference call may include many of the features of face-to-face negotiation, bargaining by email can be very different, demanding a new set of skills. As you may have to bargain by email as often as you do face to face, it's worthwhile examining how to make the most of this medium.

How much should you carry out by email?

While there is much to be said for having a written record of *everything* said in a negotiation, there is an argument for carrying out the Explain and Explore Stages face to face (or on Skype) to prevent the repeated writing and responding to exploratory questions which may tempt you into skipping these stages. An initial meeting also reveals the personalities you're dealing with, and the body language that accompanies what's said – things you won't see in an email later. This means that you can concentrate on the Propose, and – most importantly – the Bargain Stage, on email.

Tips for successful email bargaining

Be clear and polite

Without the supporting information of body language, tone of voice, and facial expression, be careful that you write exactly what you mean and that it can only be interpreted in one way – the way you intend. Strive for clarity. Avoid idioms (sayings) and humour; both can be misunderstood or cause offence. Never write in anger. If you feel strongly about something, draft an email and sleep on it before sending.

Be correct

Proof your emails thoroughly before you send them. Check spelling and grammar closely. Double-check that you have spelt the other party's name correctly. Be especially vigilant when writing numbers or you may agree to something you can't afford.

Be professional

Just because you're bargaining by email doesn't mean it's acceptable to drop into text-speak or add smileys. Adopt a professional tone and keep it consistent throughout the bargaining process, unless you want to make a specific point by changing your tone. Shifting up or down a degree of formality can have impact: if you write 'We just can't agree to that. We'll have to rethink' when you've been writing 'cannot' and 'we will' consistently, the shift will make your response stand out.

Use good email 'housekeeping'

Ensure that your email subject headers reflect where you are in the bargaining process. Don't just leave the original subject header unchanged throughout the developing negotiation. Beware of adding lengthy replies onto already extensive emails: many spam filters will block over-long emails, causing confusion and delay.

Strategies to get email bargaining back on track

People are busy and it's all too easy to lose the human touch when you're writing frequent emails trying to bargain on a specific point of negotiations. Here's how to prevent losing rapport with your opposite party:

Invest time in a pleasant greeting and sign off – every time

You'd do it if you were meeting face to face, so no matter how busy you are, take care to add just a few words of greeting and closure to your emails.

If you receive an aggressive email, don't respond in kind

Instead send a prompt and benign email of concern and suggest a face-to-face meeting to address things in person.

If you reach a stalemate where you just can't move forward

It's time to meet face to face; email is clearly compromising your creativity. Send an email or pick up the phone to suggest a meeting and some old-fashioned paper-and-pencil brainstorming.

A bargaining email: Business writing

Let's take a closer look at how a bargaining email might look in reality.

To: sdfuller@T17nmail.com

From: dtodd@45nmail.com

Subject: Promotion Negotiations, Re: Car allowance offer of 17 July 2014

Dear Simon,

I hope you had a good weekend.

Thanks for your email of 17 July in which you offer £150 a month car allowance; I have considered this at length. If, however, you could agree to an increased allowance of £200 per month, I would then be willing to work weekends when required – something I know you are keen to introduce. This increased allowance would open up better car options for me, making frequent travel to and from Head Office straightforward, facilitating weekend work, and widening our client base.

I will be out of the office tomorrow, but look forward to hearing from you soon.

With best regards,

Dominic Todd

What does this email do right?

■ Its subject header is updated, specifying which element of a wider negotiation is being discussed.

■ It states exactly what the email is replying to, even including the date of the specific email in question for easy reference.

■ It makes a succinct counter-bargain, explaining the mutual benefits of this preferred solution.

■ It sets expectations, making clear that Dominic will be unable to respond the next day, and that Simon should reply.

■ It is polite, professional, clear and warm.

Key take-aways

Write down the things you will take away from Step 4 and how you will implement them.

Topic	Take-away	Implementation
Understanding the basics of making proposals	• *Rule 1: Make your initial proposals on the basis of what you identified in the Explore Stage.* • *Rule 2: Allow the other side to make counter proposals.* • *Rule 3: Sell the benefits of the proposal to the other side.* • *Rule 4: Explain the benefits of the proposal for you.*	• *Draft a proposal and have a go at rehearsing it.* • *Think about how I would respond to an initial proposal.*
How high to pitch an opening proposal		
How to make the best of the other party opening		
How to make a counter proposal		
Understanding the basic rules of bargaining		
Knowing when to haggle		
How to haggle		
Understanding the merits of email bargaining		
How to bargain effectively on email		
How to get email bargaining back on track		

Step 5

FIND THE WIN-WIN WINDOW

'To know oneself, one should assert oneself.'
— Albert Camus, (1913–1960)
Author, Journalist, and Philosopher

Five ways to succeed

■ Separate your negotiations from the relationships involved.

■ Don't infer anything personal; always clarify what's meant.

■ Be assertive, not aggressive.

■ Always be polite.

■ Remember the other party has feelings too.

Five ways to fail

■ Use aggression to get what you want.

■ Make the other party work out the issues for you.

■ Never apologize for your mistakes.

■ Don't concern yourself with how the other party feels.

■ Never give the other party credit for good decisions.

Strictly business: nothing personal

Negotiating can be scary; no one can deny that. But perhaps one of the most effective tools you can employ to keep negotiations in perspective, and minimize the stress of them, is to remember that negotiations are 'strictly business: nothing personal', and to *keep* remembering that – especially in the middle of your negotiations. Negotiating is an everyday business process that most people will become familiar with over the course of their careers. It can and should be conducted in a way that keeps the negotiation distinct from the everyday working relationships involved. Even if the other party decides to get confrontational, resolving not to respond in kind can do much to minimize conflict. In addition, if you can make the mental leap from thinking 'the boss is going to hate me', to 'I can separate this negotiation from how I feel about the other party', then you will not only minimize your own stress, but are likely to be far more objective about everything, and may even end up with a better outcome too. Easier said than done? True, it's not easy. However, in this Step, we will be looking at effective ways to keep negotiations professional, civil, and in perspective.

The other person is not the problem

Humans have strong emotions that can often fog our judgement. When you're negotiating and things aren't going your way, it's all too easy to let frustration trample all over objectivity just when you least want it to happen. Suddenly the position of your desk next to the vending machine isn't the issue; it's your boss's inability to do anything about it. In fact, it's everything about your boss; her naff suits, the fact she has a better car than you, the way she gave Dave a promotion, even though you've been here longer ... the list goes on. Mix up your boss's actions, personality or human failings with the concrete problem of your noisy desk and you're likely to end up lashing out at the person, not the problem. Your frustration could (forgivably) be construed as a personal attack, with disastrous results: you've damaged the relationship, charged the negotiations with personal feelings, and made the whole process tense and ineffective. How do you prevent this?

■ **Keep the issue, not the person, in the front of your mind**
Before negotiating, read your strategy to remind yourself of your concrete aims. In negotiations, if you find yourself getting hot under the collar, the simple act of even writing down the reason why you're there ('pay', 'my noisy desk', 'flexible working') at the top of your notes may help anchor you in the issue, rather than in your emotions or how you feel about the person sitting opposite you.

■ **Resist confusing emotions**

The negotiation may be very important to you, but don't let your emotions get the better of you. Having done run-throughs with friends or colleagues, you will know ahead of time at which points you may start to feel upset or anxious. Take particular care at these pressure points: don't let your emotions spill out as anger or aggression. Outbursts can not only look unprofessional, but may compromise your ability to express yourself, or to digest key information. Keep yourself together, regulate your breathing, and take a sip of water to create a moment's pause if you need to. Ask for some time out or go to the restrooms to have a word with yourself; it's much better than losing your head in public. It's hard to 'come down' from an outburst with grace and credibility intact, so prevention is better than cure.

■ **Don't infer: clarify**

When we think someone is against us, we tend to pick out everything in their behaviour and language that appears to support that idea. So too with negotiations: if you're feeling defensive, you may 'read' a personal attack into what others are saying when that's not what was intended: 'I'd prefer to have you working in the office than remotely,' may sound like the boss wants to keep an eye on you, but don't immediately infer that – ask for clarification. You may discover that the boss trusts you over everyone else in his absence and there's hope for office-based flexible working or promotion.

■ **Mind your language, said and unsaid**

Are you openly complaining to colleagues about 'they' not giving 'me' what 'I' want? Not only are you being unprofessional, but your vocabulary is helping your head categorize the negotiations as something personal. If you allow yourself to think about negotiations in terms of 'them' and 'me', i.e. as a head-on conflict, then you're more likely to take the other party's objections personally, and to get pretty personal yourself. It's time to change the words your head is using from 'they' and 'me' to 'us' and 'we' and focus on the reason for your negotiation instead. Get back to your strategy, read it and think about the *issues* you want to resolve, not your gripes against the other side.

■ **Drop the mood of negotiations at the door**

When you're negotiating with a boss or a colleague, make every effort to leave your negotiation (and any disagreement) behind the minute you step out of the room or away from the table. For example, you may be negotiating a pay-rise from your boss. That does not mean that you can be surly and impolite if he/she approaches you with a reasonable request outside of the negotiation. Don't suddenly drop your 'best regards' off the end of emails to those who, at other times, you are negotiating with. Rise above the negotiations and treat them as distinct from the every day. It's not an easy thing to do, but it's professional, impressive, and will gain you respect.

Be assertive, not aggressive

Your success in negotiations depends quite simply on your being able to stick up for yourself; that is, being assertive. Being assertive means holding your corner, being rational, and not getting walked over – it's a key component of successful two-way negotiating. Assertiveness is quite distinct from aggressiveness, which is irrational, emotionally charged and often results in personal attacks. No one should resort to aggression in negotiations.

If you are someone who finds it hard to assert themselves in every-day life, it's likely that you'll also find negotiations particularly daunting, as negotiating will be a skill that won't necessarily come easily to you. But the good news is that there are several simple techniques you can adopt that will not only help you look and sound more assertive in negotiations, but will help you gain self-confidence as you go. By tweaking the way you speak and modifying your body language, you can easily adopt the behaviours of assertive people. As you make more 'little wins' using these techniques, your confidence about being assertive will grow. From repelling bullies in the playground, to securing our aims in negotiations, assertiveness is a crucial life-skill that we should all be more comfortable using – every day and at every age.

Assertive body language

In Step 2 we examined confident body language for approaching negotiations: from walking tall, to making engaged eye contact. Such confidence is the cornerstone of assertiveness, but in addition, assertive physical gestures will help emphasize your case and prevent you from falling back on aggression to make your point.

■ **Make your gestures open and calm**

Movements that are open, deliberate, and relaxed suggest control and assertiveness. When inviting the other party to speak or offering them the floor, you may, for example, extend one or both open palms in their direction – suggesting at once your control of the floor and your willingness to give it up.

■ **Use illustrative gesture**

Let your hands help to explain what you're saying. If you're explaining something in several points, count off those points on your fingers with the 'counted' palm open. If you are talking about raising standards, raise your hand in the air to indicate a visual level, and so on. These kinds of gestures are persuasive, positive, and calming.

■ **Avoid edgy, closed gestures**

Tense, fast, closed gestures look aggressive, make you feel aggressive, and will be interpreted as aggressive. They're infectious too, so avoid them. Pointing a finger or pen at others, jabbing a finger into the table for emphasis, balling your hands into a fist, or folding your arms in theatrical 'huff' are all aggressive gestures that will hint at your being emotional, irrational, and out of control.

Assertive language

At the core of assertiveness is logic: the rational interpretation and delivery of facts. So it's no surprise that to be assertive, you must *sound* logical, rational and objective. To do this you need to think about two things: what you say, and how you say them.

■ **Stick to the facts**

Deliver facts without attacking other people. So, instead of saying things like 'I'm going insane trying to concentrate in this bombsite of an office!' you might want to say something like 'I'm having difficulty working because of the constant noise in this office. I need a quieter desk.' By all means offer illustrative facts to support your case: 'In fact, I had to ask for quiet on four different occasions yesterday in order to make calls to our most important clients.' Delivering the facts in a rational manner will be much more compelling in the long run than trying to lay blame.

■ **Be objective**

To underline the fact that your argument is based on logic, control how much subjective language you use; that is, language that describes something in terms of how you *feel* about it. Instead of saying 'I hate my desk!' describe the objective facts of the situation e.g. 'It's very difficult to call clients without being interrupted.'

■ **Be practical**

Aggressive people make 'dead-end' rants that offer no solutions, often ending on something like 'So, what are you going to do about it?' Assertive people offer solutions and practical insights: 'If I was moved to a quieter floor, I'd be able to offer better telephone support.' If the time is right to strengthen your point, but without aggression, try shifting your 'if' into 'when': 'When I have a quieter desk, it will be easier to phone clients.'

■ **Be positive**

Be upfront and positive. Don't apologize or use tentative language. Be firm: 'Can I speak first when we meet again after lunch?' and 'I have to disagree with you on that.'

■ **Be clear**

Assertive people don't shout, but they don't mumble either. Raise your voice a fraction to give it authority, and speak a little more slowly than you would informally, to ensure that important information isn't lost.

■ **Watch your tone**

Keep your tone of voice even, and comfortably low-pitched. Voices that become high-pitched, tense or shrill all indicate aggression. Think about keeping your lungs and voice as open and relaxed as your body language.

Sounding Pro

So, how can we recognize the difference, and choose between, aggression and assertiveness in the thick of negotiations? Here are some phrases you might use and hear. Remember that to avoid aggression, you must keep your tone even and your volume controlled. Turn up the volume and the politest sentence can begin to sound confrontational.

Aggressive language	Assertive language
You're not listening to me!	*Excuse me, may I speak now?*
I'm really angry that you're objecting to my proposal.	*Could you clarify what it is about my proposal that you find unacceptable?*
What are you going to do about it?	*Can I make a suggestion about how we can solve this?*
I'm disgusted by your pay offer.	*This pay offer is unacceptable and I need to talk it over with you.*
Your project is so chaotic none of the team knows what's happening!	*Yesterday I had to ask several times for clarification on what our project objectives are. We need more guidance.*
Will you stop interrupting?	*Please let me finish.*
You're wrong!	*I have to disagree.*
Your suggestions are totally ridiculous!	*I can understand the thinking behind your suggestions, but I have to disagree. Can I explain my reasons why?*

Maintaining trust and respect

Trust and respect are borne out of treating others as you would wish to be treated. It's all too easy in negotiations to forget that the other side, no matter how tough they're playing, are humans too, and are prey to the same fears and insecurities as everyone else. To safeguard mutual trust and respect, as well as prevent everything from 'getting personal', it helps to think of everyone involved as humans first, and negotiators second. That doesn't mean making concessions to be 'kind'; it means paying attention to those small courtesies that protect our sense of self and allow you to get on with the business of negotiating.

Don't bypass polite social norms

No matter how difficult things get, don't forget those small gestures that make life less abrasive, like greeting each other, or apologizing. Every time you sit down together, or gather to negotiate, do say 'Good morning' or 'Hello again', and discuss the weather, the weekend, or shared interests. It's these small exchanges – which seem otherwise to achieve little – that keep emotions, resentments and misunderstandings in check. A shared whinge about the morning's traffic can ease frayed nerves and restore energy for continuing negotiation, as can the following.

Apologize

If you've lost your head at any point, said something out of order, or given some duff information while trying to make a point, face up to it: apologize promptly and sincerely. This basic human courtesy is a simple but powerful tool that can help restore trust and respect, no matter what the problem. Identifying a mistake, sharing it and apologizing for it will make others look at you in a new light; you'll go up in their estimations and they'll forget the error of judgement, effectively wiping the slate clean. Cover up a mistake, or ignore the fact you've just made an unacceptable personal attack, and the other party will quietly add this to their profile of you as a person and as a negotiator.

Don't hold grudges

Negotiation is a process of phases. There will be easy phases and really tough phases. If you and the other party have managed to get through a particularly challenging phase, don't jeopardize the next phase by holding a grudge about how hard those last ten minutes were. Once it's over, it's over, and it's time to move on. If you find it difficult to dust yourself off quickly, by all means ask to take a break, and be honest about your reasons why. You can do this positively by saying something like 'I found that tough going – can we take five minutes?' Chances are the opposite party are feeling the same, and you'll lose no respect by asking for time out.

Acknowledge the needs of others

As well as pointing out your own needs in a negotiation, acknowledge the needs of others. If you're leading negotiations and have just worked through a particularly tough point, it's a big-hearted gesture to offer the other side some time out: 'Wow, I'm tired now, are you? I think we should take a break for 15 minutes, don't you?' In this way, you can negotiate hard on the issues, but go easy on the person, maintaining a relationship of trust and mutual respect despite some really challenging moments.

Acknowledge the feelings of others

Although we've talked about avoiding language based on how you feel about something, e.g. 'I'm so angry that she was promoted over me!', it doesn't mean that you can't talk about feelings in a professional way. In fact, allowing others to explain what they're feeling can help restore trust and respect if it's handled calmly. You might say 'I'm sure that you feel upset that Sandra was promoted; after all, you've been here longer and have a lot of experience.' That gives the other person a chance to talk about their feelings rationally, rather than have to make an explosive outburst to express themselves. While an unscheduled outburst is rarely productive, a calm investigation of a person's feelings can be fruitful – it may even reveal an underlying interest that could be addressed. Perhaps, for example, your boss is reluctant to grant you flexi-time because he/she's seen the concession abused in the past.

Give credit where it's due

We all want to feel like valuable human beings, and even in the midst of negotiations, people want to feel like they're worthwhile – especially if the negotiations are hard or not going their way. So, if someone has come up with a good idea or makes a concession that eases the way for both parties, then it should be given credit. Giving credit will not only keep relations trusting and respectful, but it can help get others into the mindset of making more concessions to reach a mutually beneficial agreement: 'Thanks to you agreeing to a car allowance, I'll be much more mobile, so perhaps we could we also talk about flexible working?' By publicly giving credit for an idea or a concession, you give that person a stake in the success of a larger outcome, which means they're more likely to strive for it.

Respect other people's sense of self-worth

We all have an idea in our minds of what we are: 'a good team leader'; 'brilliant with numbers' etc. One of the tough things about negotiation is that parts of your work identity, or the work identities of others, may come under scrutiny. You may hear, or have to say, things like 'I'd give you a promotion, but I don't feel that you're up to managing more staff yet.' Ouch. If you pride yourself on being a great team leader then that may feel like a body blow, and you may feel personally attacked. If you're on the receiving end of information like this, try to get it in perspective: you are not wholly worthless or incompetent, and your boss is not getting personal. It's simply your people management skills that need more development, so don't lash out against a perceived character assassination. If you have to give out information like this, be sensitive to the fact that the other party may be feeling their sense of worth wobble under the strain.

To maintain trust and respect throughout such necessarily tough negotiations, it's helpful to protect and promote the other person's sense of self-worth. You may find this especially useful if you're negotiating with a colleague; say, over who's going to lead a project. If you're pretty sure you don't want them to lead the project then you'll have to emphasize their other business skills if you hope to keep them on side.

Breaking down the feeling of a 'head to head'

Negotiations vary; some are straightforward, with like-minded parties coming together to work towards an immediately obvious and mutually beneficial solution to a problem. Other negotiations are harder, with two opposing parties coming reluctantly together to thrash out what immediately appears to be irreconcilable differences. While there isn't scope in this step to comprehensively explain how to bring conflicting interests together, there are a number of tactics which can immediately break down the feeling of a head to head, and create a sense of shared responsibility, despite your differences. By underlining the shared nature of negotiations, you may well bring an initially obstructive opposite party on-side, making forward progress much easier.

Frequently recap on what the other side has told you

Even if you're clear on what the other side's interests are, take time to repeat these back as you understand them. It's a tactic that friends use when they don't have a solution to another's problem but want to demonstrate empathy and support. If you take a moment to say 'So this is how I understand it – you feel you need more training to support your project management – am I right?' By recapping, you demonstrate that you are careful to understand their needs, which will motivate them to understand yours.

Celebrate what you do agree on

Conflict tends to underline perceived differences and make us forget about our similarities, so you may have to spend some time emphasizing what you do share, and what you do agree on – even if that's simply the fact that you both agreed to negotiate. At the beginning of each new point of discussion, positively reiterate what you have achieved already – even if that's not very much. 'Well, that's good. We're agreed that we have to resolve this. We've now got a proper insight into what everyone hopes to achieve.' Use small 'celebrations' to create a sense of inclusion working forward, and be inexhaustibly positive: 'With all this information we've uncovered, I'm sure we can resolve things.' You may also acknowledge that your motivations (although bringing you into opposition) may actually be the same: 'We're both worried about money, that is, my salary and your overheads – let's try to work something out together.'

Talk about the future

Instead of dwelling on the past (you will have examined the history of any disagreements in the Explore phase), try to talk about the future. Don't go over things that have historically brought you here, or cast up comments that have been made in the heat of the moment earlier in negotiations. Instead, emphasise progress towards a future, shared goal: 'We've agreed on a couple of points now, let's work together on these last few issues' or 'Things will be much better when we've reached resolution on this.'

Involve the other party in the detail

We tend to value things more when we've had to work for them – saving for a holiday or a new car gives the end result an added shine. So too with negotiations: as we mentioned in Step 3, the other party is far more likely to respond positively if they feel they've had some involvement in the fabric of the agreement. This tactic is worth remembering at any difficult stage of negotiations: involvement can cast a rosy glow over the end result that would be missing if a done deal were presented without consultation. So, instead of sparing the other party the nitty gritty involved in getting to agreement, involve them. If, for example, you want your boss to fund extra training for you, ask early for advice on what skills they think you lack, or ask for recommendations on training companies they've used in the past – even though you may already know what training you want and where. Consultation at an early stage lets others leave a mark on the process that gives them a sense of investment in the outcome. Involvement also means they may later claim credit for any beneficial legacy of the negotiations, something which might be very important, for example, to your boss, and may add some motivation to agree. Letting them take credit for 're-prioritizing training' to their own superiors even when it's you who requested it will help them justify your expenses, and, in the long run, is no skin off your nose.

Change your seating

If all else fails, and the two parties remain grimly head to head, it may be time to change your seating. Create a believable reason to do this, such as, 'Can I just show you the points in my terms and conditions that I'm worried about?' or 'Can I quickly show you where my desk is in the office floor plan?' Something about the simple act of scooting a chair round 90 degrees and pulling it up to the table beside someone creates a sense of fresh start and teamwork. If there are teams involved, clear the debris from another tabletop and ask them to gather round something that is emblematic of the issues – a floor layout for an office move for example. You may have seen your boss use this tactic to bolster enthusiasm for a difficult project – there's no reason why you can't use it yourself.

Key take-aways

Write down the things you will take away from Step 5 and how you will implement them.

Topic	Take-away	Implementation
How to separate negotiations from the relationships involved	• *Keep the negotiations strategy in mind at all times.* • *Don't get emotional.* • *Watch my vocabulary.* • *Leave the negotiation behind when I leave the room.*	• *Re-read my negotiations strategy — even in the meeting.* • *Try to be aware of the areas where I might get emotional or angry.*
Being assertive not aggressive		
How to maintain trust and respect in tough negotiations		
How to break down the feeling of a head to head conflict		

Step 6

DEAL WITH DIFFICULT MOMENTS

'Be sure you put your feet in the right place, then stand firm.' — Abraham Lincoln, President of the United States (1861–1865).

Five ways to succeed

- Note significant shifts in others' body language.
- Allow difficult people to shout themselves out.
- Take control of the pace if you're being rushed or stalled.
- If you need to walk away, prepare the other party.
- Postpone negotiating further if everyone is getting tired.

Five ways to fail

- Retaliate strongly when people are aggressive to you.
- Always try to silence difficult people.
- If you don't know what to say, it's okay to walk away.
- Use breaks to talk 'off-record' to the other party.
- Never use a neutral third party to facilitate negotiations.

The tough moments

In the previous step we looked at ways to minimize any feelings of conflict between negotiating parties, and how to create a sense of shared responsibility. The techniques we examined there will stand you in good stead, but what if they're simply not enough? What if you lose the goodwill of the other party during negotiations? In this step we'll find ways to anticipate and pre-empt problems. And what if the other party is ill-tempered and abrasive from the outset? We'll also look at dealing with people who're just plain difficult from the word go. Despite our best efforts, occasionally, negotiations fail. Sometimes it's right to walk away, and we'll examine how to do so with credibility intact. We'll also explore the advantages of mediation, the best time to use it, and what you can expect from it.

Sometimes negotiations can break down because of cultural differences. Following the advice in this chapter will help get negotiations back on track and keep them there, but if you intend to undertake regular intercultural negotiations, you may need more information. There are many books on intercultural communication and etiquette which will help you negotiate more effectively – take time to research, as preparation will be key to the success for your negotiations.

Being aware of body language

Information is power, and lots of information is communicated through non-verbal communication – body language. By paying attention to the opposite party's body language, you can better identify how they're feeling at specific points, which may help you avert problems before they arise, or even gain a competitive edge. So how do you become a better interpreter of other people's body language?

Watch them off-duty

Arriving in good time for your negotiations can be crucial. Watching people when they're 'off-duty' gives you a sense of their normal, relaxed, body language. Are they animated? Do they smile easily? Do they have a loose, confident posture? Or do they seem fidgety by nature? Observing others outside of negotiations creates a benchmark against which you can compare potentially significant changes in their 'in-negotiation' body language. If a normally smiley, open-gestured person becomes fidgety, restless and prone to nervous tics, you could surmise that they're finding this negotiation difficult. You might use this non-verbal information as a cue to ask if there's anything in what you've just said that particularly concerns them. There might be something lying behind the body language that needs to be aired if you're going to stay on track.

Keep things in perspective

Don't try to see meaning in every twitch or fidget. Look around for a probable explanation, rather than jumping to conclusions. Perhaps the other party has just had a big lunch, and feels a bit tight at the waistband? Are they sitting beside a super-hot radiator? Suddenly the fact that they're perspiring isn't so significant. It's more informative to note when a *number* of elements of body language corroborate: did the other party drop eye contact, fold their arms, turn one shoulder away, then start massaging their neck? When several gestures underline one consistent message, such as 'I'm overwhelmed, I want to get out of here', *then* you have a case for taking action. You might want to pre-empt problems by offering a few minutes' break, or asking tactfully whether they have a particular concern they want to share, by saying something like 'I think something I've said may be concerning you, would you like us to talk over any worries you have?'

Don't get distracted

Don't miss opportunities for observation. If the other party is making a presentation, scan the room discreetly now and again to watch faces and note reactions. If the other party gives you paperwork, resist the temptation to bury your head in it. You might ask them to talk you through it, or give you a summary of the important points, freeing you up to stay observant as well as learn what you can from how they deliver what they have to say.

Watch out for group body language shifts

Mirroring, the subtle copying of body language between people, can be a particularly useful behaviour to look for in team negotiations. If you suddenly see a number of members of the opposing party unconsciously exhibiting consistent shifts in body language, then you may be right to surmise that a) what you've just said has had an impact, either good or bad, and b) the opposing team is pretty united. When people unconsciously adopt similar body language to each other, it's clear that they're feeling similar emotions, know each other well, and are – to an extent – in tune with one another. You may also use this non-verbal communication to note disagreement within the other team – do three members sit forward eagerly, making eye contact with you, while another drops eye contact and drums his fingers? If he's the team leader, you may still have a job on your hands to bring him on side.

Dealing with difficult people

Add a difficult person into already difficult negotiations and there's scope for some inflammatory exchanges. So how can you cope with a difficult person and still try to safeguard the negotiation at the same time?

First identify why they are difficult

Observe your abrasive opponent carefully and consider what's behind their behaviour. Is this their adopted negotiating style that they assume like a cloak at the door? Is this cold demeanour a tactic they're using to intimidate you? Be aware of indicative changes between their on- and off-duty personas. Perhaps there's something happening in their personal life at the moment? It's always best to find out in advance if you're going to be dealing with a difficult person. If possible, ask trusted colleagues about the person you'll be dealing with. Of course, that's not always possible, so you may have to resort to finding out on the hoof. Tactful questions during the negotiation will help, such as 'I can see you feel strongly about this. Can I ask what concerns you most?' Getting a handle on why this person is being mean can help you cope, and help you brush off any personal attacks with your self-esteem intact.

Don't respond in kind

If people are aggressive we often want to hit back. However, that may make things worse, and in business, could result in negotiations breaking down. If someone is being difficult with you, the best way to handle them is to be remain calm, firm, and pleasant. Never lash out in response to a personal attack. Instead, take it quietly, demonstrating self-control and dignity. You might even want to adopt the tactic of nodding benignly while the other person rants – politicians often use this tactic when faced with opposition. The incongruous nod is unsettling for the aggressor, who will often stumble towards an embarrassed halt without putting their finger on why. How else can you handle aggression without retaliation?

Encourage them to vent

They say the best correction for horses who bolt is to run them to exhaustion every time they do it, and it's a principle that works in negotiations too. If the opposite party starts on an aggressive tirade, don't try to silence them, but let them run it off instead. Offer verbal nods such as 'Go on' and 'I see' to underline your full attention. Ask them to expand with brief open questions such as 'And how does that make you feel?' or 'In what way?' until they've exhausted both their energy and their argument. This tactic can have a very clearing effect. The other person may gain release from venting their frustration and you both may well uncover something new that could provide material with which to negotiate.

Don't counter-attack; ask questions

The active listening skills we learned in Step 3 can help you deal with aggressive people. Say you've just tried to sell the benefits of a proposal and they retort with something like 'Giving you a company car will waste my time and money', resist a pantomime squabble of 'No it won't!', but instead, ask them to elaborate: 'In what ways will it be a waste?' You're likely to reveal some of their motivations for disagreement, while they're likely to identify flaws in their own argument – without personal conflict between you.

Create a bell-jar for yourself

When all else fails, a little visualization won't go amiss when you need to keep calm. Imagine yourself in negotiations with this person, but a large bell-jar placed over you protects you from their aggression. Listen to their disagreeable remarks pinging off the glass without any effect. It sounds odd, but it works.

Coping with power games

As we saw in Step 3, learning to understand where you are in the process of negotiation can help you identify if you're being rushed towards a decision, or deliberately stalled. Both tactics may be used by difficult people to get what they want. So what should you do in response?

Being rushed

If you're being pushed with closing language like 'Well, I think we are all agreed then ...' or with threatening language like 'If you don't agree now then the deal is off,' then stop the train. Make an unapologetic statement such as 'I'm not ready to agree on that.' Then explain why: 'We still need to address issues one, two and three.' If you're pushed again, be open about what's happening: 'I'm being rushed towards a decision that hasn't been properly discussed. I'd like to take a break.' As well as planning how to get the opposite party back onto the subjects important to you, use your break to compare where you are, relative to your BATNA and walk-away points (see Step 2), just in case. A rushed agreement could be worse than no agreement, so consider these fall-back positions against where you are now.

Being stalled

The other party is avoiding a topic important to you, or getting bogged down in detail to drag things out. People may stall for any number of legitimate reasons – to get more information, to get agreement from an absent authority, or to consider their position. But when stalling becomes frequent or unexplained, and starts to test your endurance, then it has become unacceptable. So how do you deal with it?

Remind the other party that both of you stand to benefit from the negotiation. To engage interest, you may have to provide an incentive. 'Could we get on to the subject of the car allowance now? When we can agree on that I can start getting out and about to drum up new clients.' On the other hand, you may also highlight the cost of not negotiating: 'If I'm not funded for the IT training next month, we'll have to renew the contract to outsource IT again, and their prices have gone up.' When all else fails, the same response applies as it would if you're being rushed – state your intent clearly, firmly and assertively: 'I feel that I'm being stalled on this issue, and would like to discuss it now.' If the other party is still evasive, it's time to ask them outright if there is something behind their reluctance to talk about it: 'Can I ask if there is something about this issue that concerns you?' Only with clear information can you get to the motivation behind stalling.

When and how to walk away

The ability to walk away on your own terms is possibly the most empowering factor in your whole negotiations strategy, giving your position security and leverage. If you have a well-defined BATNA you will also have feasible options other than negotiating to fall back on. In short, options make you look and feel less desperate. A clear walk-away point is your assurance that you cannot possibly leave worse off than when you entered.

Don't walk just because you're stuck for words

It may sound over-simplistic, but don't walk away until you reach your walk-away point. It may feel instinctive to 'bolt' from a challenging negotiation if you're feeling a bit overwhelmed, but doing so is a waste of effort and may damage your credibility. If you feel like a rabbit caught in headlights, it may be time to ask for some time out, rather than chuck the whole thing in.

There are instances when walking away ahead of schedule is an acceptable last resort: if the other party is being unethical or openly bullying, it's unlikely that you'll emerge unscathed, so you may forgivably decide to cut your losses and leave.

Don't just disappear

Though it might feel good to shuffle your papers together, grab your coat and walk out the door without a word, you may be burning bridges between you and the opposite party that you later wished you hadn't. If you *want* to have a continuing relationship with the other party – for example, if they're a client – you're unlikely to regain their full trust for some time if you walk out without warning. If you *have* to have a continuing relationship with the other party – if he/she's your colleague or boss for example – then things are going to be even harder to retrieve, and working in the office could be icy for some time. You probably don't want that. If you intend to walk away, you must first consider the options you have after doing so, and the context in which you're doing it – in other words, what will the consequences be?

Prepare them for your walk away

A far better exit strategy is to prepare the other party for your likely departure from negotiations. By giving fair and honest signals that you're now considering walking away from the negotiation, you'll have much more material with which to open dialogue at a later date, should you hope to rebuild the relationship. If you've genuinely reached the point at which you have promised yourself to walk away, come clean with this information and tell the other party about it. Ask them what both of you can do to prevent this moment becoming a deal-breaker. If they provide you with some options, do give them proper consideration, but don't be tempted to cave on your walk-away point when you have held out thus far.

If you're being forced to walk away by the unacceptable behaviour of an individual or, indeed, a team, you must similarly prepare the other party for your exit by letting them know you're unhappy with how things are unfolding. Begin with explaining that you feel their behaviour is unacceptable. If you're feeling rushed or manipulated you could say 'I feel that I'm being forced into agreeing to these terms.' If they don't behave, then you can, as a last resort, state that you'll leave the negotiation if things don't improve. Don't do this lightly; it is a threat, and you must be prepared to follow through with it or you will look foolish.

What to do it if all breaks down

Not all negotiations will achieve success in reaching an agreement – any agreement. The reasons for this can be many: perhaps the two parties have very fixed positions and are unwilling to budge on them; perhaps there is a lack of trust between the two parties. Simply failing to listen to each other, or even failing to agree on how the negotiations will be conducted, and in what timescales, can lead to deadlock or impasse. But what do you do in these situations?

Suggest a postponement

If you've been negotiating for some time and both parties are exhausted, it's not uncommon for a deadlock to be reached – it's hard to be creative when you're dog tired, and even harder to stay logical, reasonable and courteous. In such situations, there's a lot to be said for speaking up and suggesting both parties just leave the negotiations as is, and arrange to return at a later date – no one has walked away: you just 'stop'. Suggest that you break for a couple of days to think about how to get out of this deadlock. Even a good night's sleep may be enough to clear your heads and come up with some fresh ideas.

Try some brainstorming

If negotiations have been lacking in ideas, and have ground to an unrewarding halt, it may be time to reconvene and consider brainstorming some fresh ideas. If you've been negotiating one to one, enlist the help of a couple of friends or colleagues. If you're part of a team, then gather some or all of them in a setting away from the negotiation. Now is the time to change the focus from negotiating a solution to just simply getting some ideas on the table. Brainstorming focuses energy on coming up with new ideas, without fear of criticism from the other side, without fear of being judged, and without fear of sharing confidential information. Only once all ideas are aired and recorded as a collective effort should a process of evaluation begin. Then you can go back to the negotiating table with a handful of fresh and hopefully workable ideas.

Where both sides have too much invested to risk deadlock or breakdown, you may even consider brainstorming with the opposition. Not for the faint-hearted, but perhaps a better alternative than no agreement at all.

Reduce the numbers

Team negotiation can be helpful for creating ideas, gathering information, and for strength in numbers. However, teams can make swift decision-making difficult. If negotiations grind to a halt because the numbers involved are unwieldy, there may be scope for suggesting to the other party that you reduce numbers on both sides and reconvene, even down to negotiating one to one.

Change the setting

You've reached an impasse. The room is getting pretty stale, just like your thinking. When negotiations grind to a halt with both sides planting their feet and too much invested to walk away, it may be time for a change of surroundings. If you've been negotiating in one or other of your offices, there may be value in suggesting you stop negotiations and reconvene somewhere neutral. In this case, the less formal the environment the better; a relaxed context will encourage both parties to chill out a bit, which may be enough to encourage some fresh thinking, or regain an element of goodwill.

Make use of informal moments

If reconvening somewhere new is out of the question, make use of any off-duty moments you have with the other party to re-establish rapport and try for a brief, informal chat about the points you're negotiating. Use coffee or lunch breaks to approach the other party, or a member of their team. Begin just by forgetting grudges, opening (any) dialogue and attempting to re-establish the relationship e.g. 'It's been tough going in there hasn't it?' Doing so can provide both of you with an opportunity to be frank, and a bit more human too. Informality and openness may be all you need to re-establish communication and a path forward. It's good to talk, but do remember that what you say is never 'off-record': never share anything that you wouldn't divulge inside the negotiations, or you could find it used against you.

Coping with failure

The negotiation has failed and you've had to walk away. You'll be feeling disappointed, and worried about the ongoing relationship. How can you get things in perspective?

It's okay to say 'no'

If you're abiding by basic ethical and moral standards, then it's your right to say 'no'. Someone who says 'yes' to avoid conflict risks exploitation. Isn't it the people who are able to say 'no' in the right context and in the right way that we respect most? By saying 'no' to one negotiation, you may create greater leverage for yourself for another day.

It's not one person's fault

It takes two to tango, and two parties to have a failed negotiation. The breakdown of a negotiation is not solely your responsibility. There will have been at least two intelligent and responsible adults involved, so don't lie awake at night over it. Relationships continue and are reparable. If you've been courteous, honest and fair, you have nothing to fear from the on-going relationships. The credibility you've gained from staying true to yourself and your walk-away points may prove valuable: perhaps both parties may reconvene for a fresh negotiating attempt after a few weeks' breather.

Using mediators and arbitrators

In some instances, negotiations will irretrievably break down, to the extent that the parties involved refuse to negotiate further, and perhaps may be unable even to speak to each other with any semblance of civility. In such cases, they may decide to enlist the help of a third-party arbitrator or mediator.

Arbitration

When negotiating parties refer their case to an arbitrator, this third party will review all information and make an objective decision based on it. In many cases, the arbitrator will be a representative of a company's HR Department, resolving issues between employees and their line managers, or between employees and their employing company. Arbitration is voluntary, so both sides must at least be able to agree that they need arbitration and that they'll accept the final decision. This decision is usually binding and enforceable. Arbitration is conducted privately between the arbitrator and the two parties, often avoiding the need for stressful and expensive employment tribunals.

Arbitration and arbitration advice is often provided free of charge by government organisations – use the internet to find out about options in your area. In the UK this kind of advice is currently offered by ACAS (Advisory, Conciliation and Arbitration Service).

Mediation

In mediation, both parties refer their unresolved issues to a third-party mediator, who will help them reach a mutually acceptable agreement. In many small disputes, the role of objective mediator could be fulfilled simply by a colleague from another office, or a representative from HR. A mediator makes no decisions or judgements, but instead gets both sides talking again, so that they may achieve resolution themselves. If the parties feel unable to negotiate in person for example, mediators may even act as spokesperson or go-between, and suggest ways to repair working relationships. Anyone can be a mediator, because, unlike arbitration, mediation has no binding element to administer. However, mediators should be chosen carefully, with the full agreement of both parties. Like arbitration, formal mediation services are often offered free of charge by government organizations. In the UK, ACAS is perhaps the best-known resource for employers and employees to consult for help and advice.

Mediation and arbitration are incredibly valuable resources, with high success rates in both large- and small-scale disputes. However, they *are* a last resort, and should only be considered when you've exhausted all other avenues to reach a resolution. By referring your case to a third party, both parties must agree to let go of some, if not all, control of the negotiation, which can be difficult. Therefore, before you consider arbitration or mediation, do try to resolve conflict using internal procedures, and by taking advice from trusted sources, such as your HR Department, line manager or union representative.

Key take-aways

Write down the things you will take away from Step 6 and how you will implement them.

Topic	Take-away	Implementation
How to interpret body language in order to pre-empt problems	• *Watch the other party off duty.* • *Pay attention.* • *Don't infer too much.* • *Watch out for group behaviour.*	• *Be more aware at next team meeting.* • *During negotiations ask others to read out handouts for the team.*
How to deal with difficult people		
How to cope with power games like rushing or stalling		
Knowing when and how to walk away from negotiations		
What to do if it all breaks down		
Coping with failure		
Using mediators and arbitrators		

Step 7
CLOSE THE DEAL

'Unless both sides win, no agreement can be permanent.' — Jimmy Carter, President of the United States (1977–1981)

Five ways to succeed

- Record everything you agree.
- Check any term of the agreement that isn't clear.
- Ask outright if the other party seems to have a problem.
- Treat implementing the agreement as a project in itself.
- Acknowledge the completion of every action point.

Five ways to fail

- Don't let reaching agreement be held up by detail.
- Never make a late concession just to reach agreement.
- Take time out after negotiations: your work is done.
- Don't try to repair relationships bruised by negotiating.
- Never discuss past negotiations with the opposite party.

The Agree Stage

You've done your research, you've made your proposals, you've had your disagreements, and despite some nail-biting moments along the way, you are now getting tantalizingly close to a decent agreement. This is the last stage of negotiation, the Agree Stage, also known as 'the close'. It may be tempting to push through this stage quickly, cutting a few corners in order to get back to normal life and start reaping the rewards of your negotiations. In reality, the opposite is true. You must be firm, attentive and methodical throughout the Agree Stage. You must ensure that everything that you have discussed and verbally agreed, is accurately represented in the final agreement.

Getting to agreement is not simple, and you may find that to do so you have to go over the same issues a few times to reach compromise, or even put some issues to one side in order to keep making forward progress. This means that often the thorniest issues turn up again at the end. That's okay, don't be discouraged; you're on the home stretch, and this step will give you the tools to navigate this important phase.

What should happen in the Agree Stage?

These few pointers should help keep things moving to a close and minimize surprises along the way.

■ **Record any agreements**

Note-taking as you agree issues is critical to negotiation success. Now discuss those notes, ensure they correspond with everyone's expectations, and use them to formalize the agreement.

■ **Check anything that isn't clear**

You may be embarrassed to seek clarification at this late stage, but it's better to do so now than to have a term written into an agreement that you're unclear on, or are unable to accept.

■ **Don't ignore detail**

If it isn't in the final agreement it may not be done. So spell it out in black and white. It may be obvious to you that you wish to start flexible working next month, but if it's not written down, your intended start date may be delayed or ignored.

■ **Support the path to agreement**

When concluding, be supportive of the other person. People tend to remember their most recent impressions of a project, so try to close negotiations on a positive note, and so begin implementation on the right foot.

The Agree Stage can be frustrating because there's no guarantee that you'll reach agreement soon (especially if the other party is uncooperative) and yet you seem so close to reaching resolution. A linear route from proposal to agreement is rare; you may well have to consider alternatives or new ideas even at this late stage.

Sounding Pro: Closing the negotiation

So how should you go about carrying out these important points? Here are some examples of how you might raise these topics and end on a positive note.

Recording any agreements	*Let's note what we've agreed so far.*
	What are the main points that we've agreed?
	Can we just run through everything we've agreed?
Checking anything that isn't clear	*I'm sorry, I'm not clear about the dates we've agreed.*
	Could you just explain what you mean by 'extra responsibility'?
	I just need to clarify one or two things.
Reviewing alternatives and introducing new ideas	*As I see it, there are two alternatives.*
	Could I make a quick suggestion about how we could finally resolve this?
Being positive	*There are very few points left to resolve before we reach agreement.*
	Things will be much better for us both when we've reached an agreement on this.
Agreeing	*Are we all agreed then? Have we covered everything?*
	Thank you everyone, I believe we've reached an agreement.

Last-minute problems

At the end of a negotiation you have reached an agreement in principle. What do you do if a last-minute problem arises? How do you deal with it? There are several things you can do, and in addition it's important to stay positive and courteous. Keep your emotions in check at this late stage, as you don't want to sour proceedings right at the last gasp. Then, fall back on the skills you've learned in Steps 5 and 6 that promote positive feeling and maintain progress:

- **Re-emphasize the benefits of the collaboration:** 'When I'm doing flexible hours I'll be able to provide holiday and absence cover for the company much more effectively.'

- **Encourage and applaud any constructive input from the other side:** 'That new office floor plan has really helped us visualize things better.'

- **Say outright that you're looking for a solution that is acceptable to both sides:** 'I want us both to gain something from this, and I think we can.'

- **Give the other side an easy route to saying yes:** 'How would it be if I liaised with HR directly over flexible working arrangements and a start date? Would that help?'

Dealing with persistent problems

Perhaps the opposite party has a problem with making the final leap to agreement, perhaps it's you. Perhaps you feel unable to deliver on the agreement terms or that your interests haven't been fully addressed. Better to act now and face the problem together than fall silent and get swept to an unsatisfactory close. Speak up, but do organise your thoughts before doing so:

■ Signal there's a problem

It may be nerve-wracking, but even at this late stage, it's better to talk about problems than agree to something you can't fulfil, or be forced to walk out because it's your only escape route – either may damage relationships in the long-term. So do broach your concerns, without apology, yet acknowledging that the timing is difficult, e.g.: 'I know it's late in the day, but I do still have a problem with one of the terms of the agreement.'

■ Explore the outcomes

Don't just dump the problem in the opposite party's lap and sit back. Proactively explore the impact of the problem, to get both sides thinking positively about solutions, and to show that you're committed to resolution. Saying something like 'What do you think will happen if we can't sort this out?' makes the problem a shared one, rather than you obstructing agreement.

■ Stay positive

Don't inject pessimism, or both of you may admit defeat. Using positive language like 'I'm sure we can sort this out,' can keep both sides motivated and remind you that agreement is within reach.

Sweeten the deal

If you've still been unable to reach agreement, last-resort tactics can help get you there. Remember that any concessions shouldn't leave you with less than your BATNA (Best Alternative to a Negotiated Agreement). Here are a few options that you may want to consider for the greater good of a satisfactory agreement:

■ Agree to 'split the difference'

Say, for example, you want flexible working from January, but your boss says wait until May. Agree on starting in March.

■ Agree a date for future talks

Sometimes it's useful to offer the other side a temporary escape route, so they can collect their thoughts or seek advice. Simply draw a line under the negotiations thus far, and arrange a date to meet again.

■ Make a late concession

Holding a small concession (say agreeing to cover a colleague's holiday absence) until the last minute can clinch a deal and make the other party feel good about 'winning'. This can also get implementation off onto the right foot, with the other party feeling satisfied rather than resentful.

Ensuring commitment to the deal

The negotiation is over. Everyone is in agreement, and you've shaken hands on it. Now the final phase begins: it's time to ensure that everyone follows through on exactly what they've agreed, with their full commitment. So how do you ensure that this happens? It is important, as part of the Agree Stage and closure of the deal, to also spend some time agreeing what the next action points are going to be.

At the end of many negotiations, and before you sign any binding agreement, it's common to write a letter of intent. This is not a legal document, but it explains what each partner intends to do and when, and in relevant cases, at what price. A letter of intent often forms the basis of a later contract. In other, less formal negotiations, the notes you have made and discussed during negotiations will be invaluable, and will eventually become your and the other party's immediate 'action points'.

No matter what the nature of the agreement you have made, it's incredibly useful to put *something* in writing immediately after the negotiation has been completed, while the agreements are still fresh in everyone's minds, and while enthusiasm and commitment levels are still high.

Business writing: a letter of intent

A letter of intent may be sent by post or email – either is appropriate. Remember that this letter will become emblematic of the negotiations (and your professional credibility) to the opposite party. It's also pivotal in creating, maintaining, or restoring a working partnership, so ensure that it's proof-read thoroughly, is grammatically sound, and perhaps most importantly, that you spell the opposite party's name correctly.

Breathing Space Air Conditioning
2 Hallhill Industrial Estate
Huntingdon, HD3 4BX

Dear Greg,

I would like to confirm my intent to offer you standard flexible working hours, subject to contract which will follow.

We agree that you will now be available for weekend working. I will ensure that this is limited only to holidays and absence cover.

We intend to begin the agreed flexible working on the 23rd September 2014. We agree that your salary and benefits package will otherwise remain unchanged.

This agreement will be subject to the results of a performance review at six months from the start of flexible working.

Please confirm that you are happy with these terms and I will forward a contract by return.

Sincerely,

Sandra Welsh
General Manager

The features of a letter of intent

While every letter of intent will be different, there are several features that will be common to most of them. Understanding these will help you write any document that agrees on a course of action after negotiation.

- **Reason for writing:** Make clear why you are writing: this is a follow up from the negotiations and is to clarify everyone's intentions after negotiating.

- **Action:** Make clear what your expectations are of the other party, and what you intend to do in return.

- **Timings:** Gives clear timescales for when things will happen. It's appropriate to note any relevant end dates too.

- **Budget:** Highlight the agreed budget for projects or fees for services. In the example on page 133, the writer notes that Greg's salary will remain unchanged.

- **Due diligence:** This term is used to describe the checking of a business or person prior to signing a contract, or acting with a certain standard of care. In this example, both parties have agreed on a performance review to ensure everything goes well.

- **The next steps:** Make clear what you want the other party to do, or describe what should happen next.

Even if your negotiation was an informal one, these headers will make you think about important aspects you should mention in any written follow-up.

Commitment to the agreement

As important as written communication, letters of intent and contracts are, it is imperative to safeguard commitment to the agreement by paying attention to the mood of the new relationship too.

■ **Show your enthusiasm**

Even if negotiations have been difficult, show that you're 'over it' by making prompt contact with the other side and agreeing action points by phone or email.

■ **Open up two-way communication**

If all the communications seem to be coming from you and you're getting little back, suggest a face-to-face meeting to re-establish a two-way exchange and talk openly about any problems.

■ **Keep communications concise**

Keep initial communications concise and make acting on them straightforward. If you burden the other party upfront with complicated details that create extra work, you'll risk sluggish replies and a loss of interest in the agreement.

■ **Follow through on promises**

If you've said you will do something or will provide something by a certain date, deliver it and on time. Be reliable. It will encourage reciprocal behaviour, creating mutual respect, teamwork, and momentum. If you can't do something in the timescales expected, be honest about it early so that contingency plans can be made.

Implementing the agreement

You are now entering a new phase: implementation. By all means celebrate the end of negotiations and enjoy a well-deserved breather, but don't take your eye off the ball for too long, or the terms for which you both worked so hard may not be properly fulfilled.

■ Recognize that implementation is a project too

The implementation demands commitment, reliability and drive to maintain momentum and ensure each of the agreement terms is delivered to mutual satisfaction. Set timescales for completion and agree them with the other party.

■ Decide whether someone needs to lead it

Identify whether anyone from either of the two parties is going to lead the implementation process and how they will consult with others on its progress. Having a clear leadership can help maintain momentum, but it must involve others in its decisions.

■ Create a schedule of actions

When you're working on action points from the agreement, set yourself deadlines and let the other party know what these are. Sharing deadlines manages expectations and creates a feeling of teamwork.

■ Offer to share jobs

Show your commitment to the implementation and to the partnership by offering to share action points and workload where appropriate.

■ Make time for each other

Make time to schedule occasional face-to-face meetings, and try to vary location. Meeting in both workplaces, and outside them, will underline a sense of equality and teamwork.

Repairing or restoring relationships

Negotiations can be hard, and sometimes relationships can become bruised by the experience, despite the fact that agreement may have been reached. Things can be even harder if negotiations have broken down entirely and both parties are left adrift with no clear route forward. So how do you restore these relationships so that you can get back to working together smoothly?

Communicate with sensitivity

Previously we talked about how to ensure commitment to your deal by communicating action points promptly after negotiating. This exchange will be the first step in restoring mutual trust, so be careful what you write and how you write them if things are sensitive between you. Pay attention to social detail in letters and emails: if you're writing on a Monday, start your email with 'I hope you had a good weekend', and never drop a courteous sign-off, even if you're busy. If the other party fulfils an action point for you, acknowledge it: 'Thanks for sending me through the contracts so promptly – it has really helped to get things moving.' Acknowledge and congratulate each fulfilment of the terms of the agreement, as they happen.

Meet on neutral territory

When repairing a relationship after a successful negotiation, meeting somewhere neutral – away from both your places of work – can be time well spent. If it's a colleague or your boss you're dealing with, suggesting a coffee at the end of the day and away from the office may build bridges. Be honest about why you want to meet: 'I think it would be good to catch up again after the negotiation.' If you're reconnecting with someone outside your place of work, pick up the phone and be upfront: 'Look, I know things got really tough last week, so I wondered whether we might meet up and talk things over? It would be good to catch up.' When you do meet, dress down a bit and leave your briefcase in the office. Make it clear this isn't another tough negotiation but a chance to talk as people first.

Talk about the negotiation

When the two of you are face to face, you can start to open up the topic of the past negotiation. Using your active listening skills from Step 3, encourage the other party to talk, supporting them with open questions and verbal nods. An opening question such as 'How do you think the negotiations went?' or 'What did you think about the negotiations?' gives the other party a blank canvas to talk about any aspect of the negotiations that they're still thinking about. Things may still be emotionally charged, so remember the skills you learned in Step 5 to defuse aggression if it does creep in. However, by choosing the neutral surroundings of a café or restaurant, you will not only help the other party relax, it's also less likely that they'll make an outburst in such a public place.

Don't apologize for negotiating

During your meeting, and in any written communication you have with the opposite party, it's good to be sensitive – to show your 'human side' – which you may have kept in check during negotiations. However, you needn't apologize *for* negotiating: remember that your reasons for negotiating were valid and pressing, and you have not solely created tension in your relationship with the other party. If you were 'out of order' at any point during negotiations, by all means make a specific apology about that, but distinguish apologizing for a brief error of judgment during negotiations from the wider need for negotiating in the first place.

Promote the other party to 'ally' status

If you're now on speaking terms with the other party, and really do want to invest in the relationship, carefully consider giving them a vote of confidence by asking them to connect on the networking website LinkedIn®. By doing so, you are effectively saying 'I trust you and want you to be a business ally for the long run.' If you are already connected on LinkedIn® or other social media such as Facebook and Twitter, start making a conscious effort to attend to that online relationship a bit more actively, to show that you have a renewed interest in, and connection with, the other party (and bear no grudges!). LinkedIn® and other social media, when used appropriately, can strengthen connections over time by highlighting shared interests and aspirations, and by enabling regular, positive contact in a convenient and unobtrusive manner:

■ **React to their profile and status updates:** If you use LinkedIn®, your daily routine may already include checking what your contacts are doing via their updates and posts. Use this information to help personalize contact with your (now former) opposite party too. So, for example, you may congratulate them within LinkedIn® on a new job status update, or start your next email to them by mentioning a post they have made. This not only makes communication easier to initiate each time, but shows you're taking an interest in the other party.

- **Post regular updates:** Share information, articles and observations with the opposite party, as a low-key way of demonstrating their importance to you. If they want to respond, they can and will.

- **Post comments or likes:** Make personal contact quickly by commenting on your opposite party's posts on LinkedIn®. If you're pushed for time, even hitting 'like' will briefly make them feel good about the fact you noticed and cared.

- **Endorse:** LinkedIn's® endorsement function allows you to attest to a contact's skills and expertise, and is something you may want to consider to build rapport between you and the other party. Use this feature only to authenticate skills that you've 'seen in action'. By endorsing judiciously, everyone wins. Your contact builds a strong and verified skills profile, you give them a useful and appropriate 'gift', and both of you feel good about the transaction.

Have patience

Time is a great healer, and if your fledgling partnership with the former opposition seems to be limping along at present, give it time. Just keep being reliable, honest and fair, and trust will follow after. Use the skills you learned in Step 5 to break down feelings of conflict and encourage a sense of teamwork: instead of having the other person come to you all the time, make the effort to go to their office or desk. Ask them for advice. Sit side by side, rather than head-on. Prioritize face-to-face meetings over email exchanges, and make time for the other party.

How did you do?

Negotiations are over, perhaps for the time being. You may be buoyed by the success of your efforts, or disappointed that negotiations broke down or that you had to walk away. If you're in the latter camp, remember that you were not the sole executor of the negotiations, so you cannot be held solely responsible for the outcome. Negotiation is a business process that has no reflection on your worth as a person. Keep things in perspective and don't lose sleep over it. Instead, think positively about all the vital skills you've learned along the way.

How to review your performance

If you're disappointed, stop brooding. If you're delighted, don't get complacent. Now is the time to promptly record any insights that you gained from your negotiations experience, while they're still fresh in your mind. If you're in a field where you think you may have to undertake negotiations frequently, perhaps if you have to work a lot with suppliers or contractors, it may well be worthwhile starting a negotiations journal. This document could include each 'case', and what you learned from it, recorded for future reference and building into your personal negotiations manual.

No matter what your circumstances, you should at least put aside some time to ask yourself some honest questions about your performance. Everyone learns from mistakes and failure, and good negotiators don't become so overnight. Think about these questions and add your own:

- What went well? Why?

- What went badly? Why?

- How could I have improved things?

- Was I well-prepared for negotiations?

- What was the biggest surprise?

- What was the most important thing I learned from this negotiation?

By undertaking an honest review of your performance you will equip yourself with the tools to do even better in the future. Negotiating is not an easy skill, but it's a valuable one, both in the office and outside it. Your efforts will not be wasted.

Key take-aways

Write down the things you will take away from Step 7 and how you will implement them.

Topic	Take-away	Implementation
How to best navigate the Agree Stage	• *Record any agreements.* • *Check anything that isn't clear.* • *Don't ignore detail.* • *Be assertive, not aggressive.*	• *Improve note-taking in meetings as practice.* • *Reread Step 5 for advice on assertiveness.*
How to deal with last-minute problems		
What to do when problems persist		
Using last resort tactics		
How to ensure commitment to the deal		
How to write a letter of intent		
Implementing the agreement		
How to repair or restore relationships after negotiating		
How to review your performance		